cat breeds

cat breeds

hamlyn **all color**

Facts, figures, and profiles of over 80 breeds

David Taylor

hamlyn

To Shelagh and in memory of Bucktooth

An Hachette UK Company
www.hachette.co.uk

First published in Great Britain in 2010 by
Hamlyn, a division of Octopus Publishing Group Ltd
Endeavour House
189 Shaftesbury Avenue
London
WC2H 8JY
www.octopusbooksusa.com

Distributed in the U.S. and Canada by Octopus Books USA:
c/o Hachette Book Group
237 Park Avenue
New York, NY 10017

ISBN 978-0-600-62094-5

Printed and bound in China

10 9 8 7 6 5 4 3 2 1

The advice in this book is provided as general information
only. It is not necessarily specific to any individual case and
is not a substitute for the guidance and advice provided by
a licensed veterinary practitioner consulted in any particular
situation. Octopus Publishing Group accepts no liability or
responsibility for any consequences resulting from the use
of or reliance upon the information contained herein.

No cats or kittens were harmed in the making of this book.

Contents

Introduction

Everyone should have a cat. They are ideal pets. They don't need exercising, as a dog does, and they generally require less space than a dog. They make excellent companions for the elderly and infirm and are easy to care for. In addition, if necessary, they can often be kept completely indoors.

There are over one hundred breeds of pedigree cat and an amazing variety of non-pedigrees. How do you decide on which one is right for you? As a first step, read on. There is a stunning gallery of cats of all kinds in the following pages.

Pedigree or not?

If you want to show or breed a cat professionally you will obviously have to buy a pedigree animal, and this can be expensive. If you cannot afford the full price you may be able to obtain a 'pet-quality' cat from a breeder, or you might be able to come to some agreement over breeding, such as letting the breeder have the pick of the first litter. You might be able to purchase a show-quality cat at a lower price and return it to the vendor at prearranged times for breeding. Any such agreement should be put in writing.

Russian Blue

When you are choosing a pedigree cat you should take into account any particular characteristics of the breed – they are described in this book – which may influence your decision. Siamese and Burmese, for example, can be demanding and loud, and they may mature more quickly than other cats. If you want find a longhaired cat appealing, think about the time you will have to spend grooming it thoroughly every day.

Non-pedigrees

What about non-pedigree cats? There are always hundreds of cross-bred felines of different types, colours and patterns needing good homes, and if your motive in obtaining a cat is as a companion-about-the-house, contact your local animal rescue centre or humane society and go along to see the cats. You are likely to fall in love with one of them, and one of them is equally likely to fall in love with you.

Male or female

In general there is nothing to choose between a castrated tom and a spayed queen. Un-neutered animals of either sex can present problems, and neutering eliminates these disadvantages, usually

Red Self Longhair (Persian)

making the cat more affectionate. Neutering also reduces behaviours such as urine spraying in male cats

Kitten or adult?

All kittens are appealing, but a kitten will need a lot of attention and have to be house-trained. On the other hand, a kitten will usually adapt quickly to its new surroundings. For many people, however, a fully grown cat is a sensible choice, particularly if you are out at work all day or would find a kitten too boisterous and time consuming to train.

The development of the modern cat

A history of cat breeds

Where did your beloved fireside familiar or, indeed, the champion of the latest national cat show come from?

Cat origins

The first true cats began to stalk the earth some 12 million years ago. Most of those original animals are long gone, but the manul or Pallas's cat (*Felis manul*), the longhaired wild cat of Asia, is still around. A contemporary of the manul, Martelli's wild cat lived all over Europe and in parts of the Middle East. It faded out around a million years ago, but many believe that it was the direct ancestor of the modern small wild cats from which domesticated cats were later to be developed.

Russian Blue

Among its descendants was *Felis silvestris*, which padded into the picture between 600,000 and 900,000 years ago. It spread all over Europe, Africa and Asia and, in due course, gave rise to three main types: the forest wild cat (*Felis silvestris*), the Asiatic desert cat (*Felis silvestris ornata*) and the African wild cat (*Felis silvestris lybica*). It is from the last of these, the African wild cat, that the domestic cat is thought principally to be descended.

Manx

Domestication

The domestication of the cat began at least 5,000 years ago, as we know from the discovery of the bones of African wild cats in the dung heaps of ancient human cave dwellings. What we don't know is whether these early humans hunted cats to eat them or to rear and tame them as companions and pest controllers.

By the time of the Ancient Egyptians, however, cats were not only employed as guardians of grain stores but also worshipped as gods. The name for these household gods was Miw, and the cats were greatly revered as supremely successful hunters that were endowed with strength, agility and lethal purpose, and their owners went into mourning when they died. The

dead cats were mummified and, after being taken to the Great Temple of the cat god Bast, Bubastis, they were buried in special cat cemeteries. Large numbers of these mummies have survived and have enabled scientists to identify this first domestic species of cat as *Felis sylvestris lybica*, the African wild cat, a species that is still abundant in all parts of Africa except the waterless deserts and depths of the equatorial forest belt.

It is believed that from about 900 BC domestic cats began to spread around the world, although some authorities put domestication in China at around 2000 BC. Other researchers, however, place it as late as AD 400.

Cat calendar

900 BC   Shorthaired cats arrive in Italy from Egypt.

AD   Shorthaired cats spread through Europe from Italy, reaching Britain by about AD 900.

16th century   Longhaired cats arrive in Italy from Turkey. Manx cats arrive on the Isle of Man on Spanish ships from the Far East.

17th century   Shorthaired cats arrive in the USA with the first settlers.

Mid 19th century Longhaired cats arrive in Britain from Turkey.

Late 19th century Longhaired cats imported into USA from Britain. Russian Blues arrive in Britain from Russia. Siamese arrive in Britain from Spain.

Late 19th century Abyssinians arrive in Britain from Abyssinia.

1920s   Birmans arrive in France from Burma.

1930s   Burmese arrive in the US from Burma.

1950s   Turkish cats arrive in Britain from Turkey. Korats imported into USA from Thailand.

1970s   Singapuras imported into US from Singapore. Angoras imported into USA from Turkey. Japanese Bobtails imported into the USA from Japan.

Birman

Blue-cream Shorthair

The box on page 12 summarizes the most important dates in the spread of cats around the world. It's important to note, however, that other types of longhaired cats were being exported over the years from Iran and Afghanistan, and many of these undoubtedly carried the blood of the manul (*Felis manul*).

Changing fortunes

In the Middle Ages the fortunes of cats changed dramatically when the Christian church, disliking their connections with witchcraft and other pagan cults, waged a campaign against them. Perhaps because of the inscrutable, knowing ways of the animal, superstitious people believed that witches could assume feline form. The result was that cats were persecuted, some even being burned alive.

Gradually, however, cats became less unpopular as their usefulness became recognized once again, and by the 18th century they were once more a familiar sight in many households.

It could be said that one of the problems with cats is that they don't *do* anything. Of course, they give pleasure by being beautiful and companionable, but they do not, unlike dogs, perform a range of specific and disparate tasks for man. For centuries dogs have been selectively bred to do many things, from retrieving game to guiding the blind and from working with the police and armed forces to herding sheep. As we all know, cats don't do much, apart from, sometimes, catching mice.

For this reason, although cats, most of them nondescript in appearance, had long been loved for their temperament, the concept of selectively breeding them to produce pedigrees did not become widely accepted until the mid-19th century. Until

Asian Self

then the appearance of most cats was the result of random, accidental matings and, from time to time, spontaneous mutations. This changed when the showing of cats started.

Showing cats

Although the first cat show on record was held as part of an English fair in 1598, the first serious showing really began only in 1871, when a large show for Persian and shorthair types was held at London's Crystal Palace. At around the same time the first American show was held in New England for the Maine Coon breed. Some early shows featured multiple judges in the ring. The idea of pedigree cats with distinct characteristics had arrived.

Cat clubs and societies began to spring up around the world, and this subsequently led to the creation in each country of a controlling authority for these organizations that would lay down formally approved standards for all

Singapura

Bombay

breeds, oversee the registration of pedigrees and the transfer of ownership, and approve show dates. In Britain, for example, there is the Governing Council of the Cat Fancy (GCCF), while in the USA the largest body is the Cat Fanciers Association (CFA).

It has been a long journey for our cats, from being worshipped as gods in Ancient Egypt, by way of the streets of New York and Paris and the dustbins of London and Sydney, to the show benches of towns and cities around the world, where champion specimens regularly fetch prices of several thousand dollars. We cat-loving owners of even the humblest kitten know it was a journey that was well worth making.

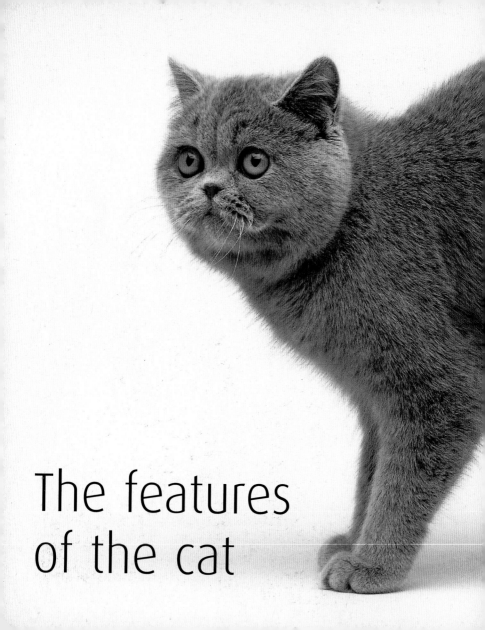

The features
of the cat

Shapes and body form

Cats, like mice and men, are mammals and possess the features common to all mammals, such as hair and mammary glands to produce milk to feed their young. The basic body pattern of all mammals, from Blue Whales to street cats to humans, is the same, and cats have tissues and organs that are fundamentally no different in structure and function from those of human beings.

Burmilla

Oriental Shorthair

There are differences, however, arising from the adaptations that have occurred in various species to suit them for their particular role in life. Humans, for example, are upright, bipedal, omnivorous primates and are equipped with the necessary specializations for such creatures. Cats are quadruped, carnivorous predators, and their anatomy is perfectly designed for the way they need to go about their business.

Blue-cream Shorthair

The design of the feline shoulder joint permits the foreleg to be turned in almost any direction. In fact, if cats were automobiles, the suspension of the feline model would give a near perfect 'ride'.

Also, unlike humans, the cat lacks a clavicle or collarbone, having instead just a small scrap of clavicle tissue deep in the breast muscle. The human collarbone allows the forearm to be lifted outwards. Cats don't require such a movement, and so this extra bone is unnecessary. In any case, a full collarbone would broaden the animal's chest, which would have the undesirable effects of reducing the cat's ability to squeeze through narrow spaces and limit the length of its stride. All in all, the feline body is capable of unrivalled fluid movement.

All cats, domestic or wild, big or small, are the same. The little tabby snoozing at your fireside is constructed in the same way as the Bengal tiger or snow leopard.

Body basics

The cat has a highly elastic body. The spine is held together by muscles, rather than ligaments as is the case in human, and there are up to 26 more vertebrae than in the human backbone. This makes the cat's back extremely flexible.

Body size and type

While domestic dogs come in a multitude of shapes and sizes, domestic cats have not been produced with much in the way of anatomical extremes. There are three main body shapes:

- Cobby
- Muscular
- Lithe

The cobby cat is a solidly built individual with short, thick legs, broad shoulders and

length, slightly rounded head. An example is the American Shorthair.

The lithe cat is lightly built with long, slim, elegant legs, narrow shoulders and rump, and a long, narrow, wedge-shaped head. An example is the Siamese.

Teeth and digestion

The cat is equipped with 24 milk teeth, which are followed by 30 permanent teeth, 16 in the upper jaw and 14 in the lower. These include the canine, or fang, teeth for biting, and specialized blade-like, carnassial molar teeth for shearing flesh. The canines in the wild animal are the main killing instrument.

Siamese

rump, and a short, rounded head with a flattish face. Examples are the various types of British Shorthair.

The muscular body type has medium-length legs, shoulders and rump that are neither wide nor narrow, and a medium-

Tortoiseshell Shorthair

The domestic cat has short sturdy jaws

Cats are more highly specialized carnivores than dogs (many of which are essentially omnivorous), and they possess alimentary tracts that are designed purely for meat eating. Consequently, the cat's intestines are proportionately shorter than those of the human or dog. It's a fascinating fact that the intestines of domestic cats are relatively longer than those of wild cats, probably because our pets have become adapted to, and fond of, the more varied, and to some extent less meaty, food that we put down for them.

The ears

The cat's skull is also notable for its large auditory *bullae* (echo chambers). These enhance the cat's sensitivity in hearing such delicate sounds as the scurrying of a mouse in the undergrowth or the rustling of a bird among leaves.

To give strength to the bite, the cat has short, sturdy jaws worked by powerful muscles that are anchored in arches of bone placed strategically on the skull. These arches reinforce all the points that are likely to come under strain when the cat bites. The teeth of the domestic cat are equipped with 'pressure feeling' nerves. When the teeth sense they are in the correct position, an ultra-fast message is sent to the jaw muscles that quickly close the jaws like a mousetrap.

As you might expect, the parts of the feline brain that are associated with the senses are well developed, as befits a skilled hunter that depends on its detection mechanisms. On the other hand, the 'intelligence' areas in the frontal lobes are much simpler than in primates, such as humans or apes, and even other highly intelligent species, like the dolphin.

The American Curl has distinctive, curled-back ears

Colours and markings

The remarkable variety of colours and coat patterns that we see today in the modern domestic cat are essentially manmade. Artificial selection by breeders, particularly in recent years in the form of 'designer cats', is responsible for it. This experimentation is set to continue.

The wild felines from which our pets are descended possess coat colours and patterns that are relatively modest by comparison with those of the domestic cat, and, crucially, those they possess serve a purpose. The markings of a tiger or wild cat provide important camouflage when they are stalking or ambushing. Black tips on tails or ears are useful for signalling to other individuals or to act as 'follow me' signs when youngsters are being led. The basic domestic cat is, or rather, was, like its forebears, a tabby. A cat that looks like a Cameo Longhair, for example, or, especially, a Sphynx, would have trouble catching its lunch when hunting in the jungle or desert. Modern cat breeding involves breeders developing coat colours and patterns that are attractive to human beings but have no biological function for the cat itself.

Nowadays a complex vocabulary is used by aficionados to denote the vast array of colours and markings sported by pedigree breeds. You will find many used in this book, so in the table on page 28 are some descriptions of them. The word 'recognized' in this context means that it is accepted by one or more cat fancies or associations.

Snowshoe

Tabby Shorthair

Colourpoint with gloves

Van pattern

Spotted Tabby/Part-colour

Silver

Common colours and markings

Bi-colour   White coat with dark patches of any recognized colour.

Blaze   A white strip down the nose (as in horses).

Calico   Also known as Tortoiseshell and White.

Cameo   A white undercoat with tipped guard hairs of some recognized colour.

Chinchilla   A pure white coat with black tipping.

Colourpoint   A white or ivory body with tail, paws, face and ears of another colour.

Dilute   A pale shade of a colour.

Harlequin   Black and white bi-colour; also known as Piebald, Magpie or Tuxedo.

Mantle   A dark topcoat above a pale undercoat.

Mitted   White paws on dark legs; also known as Gloves.

Part-colour   Bi-colours and Tortoiseshells.

Points   Coloured extremities (ears, face, nose, paws and tail).

Self   One single colour; also known as Solid.

Shaded   Medium tipping.

Shell   Light tipping.

Silver   White hairs with black or transparent tips that give a silvery effect.

Smoke   A white undercoat with a topcoat that is white at the roots and coloured at the ends; darker points on back, head and feet.

Tabby   There are four forms. **Ticked**: each hair has contrasting dark and light colour bands; **Mackerel**: vertically striped; **Spotted**: spots or blobs; **Classic**: whorls or 'oyster' marks on the sides. All have a distinct M mark on the forehead, 'spectacles' around the eyes, rings on the tail and 'broken rings' or bars on the legs.

Tipping   The guard hairs of the overcoat are coloured along some of their length.

Torbie   A mixture of tabby and tortoiseshell markings with white or cream.

Tortoiseshell   A two-coloured, black and red coat; also known as Tortie.

Van pattern   Largely white with patches of red or cream at the base of the ears and on the tail

Coats

The cat's coat is truly its crowning glory. It serves to protect and insulate the body against cold, and in the wild the colours and patterns provide camouflage. For us, the owners of domestic cats, the appearance of the coat is one of the animals' main charms, and over many centuries spontaneous colour mutations and, in more recent times, selective breeding have produced the wide variety of coats 'worn' by pedigree cats.

The domestic cat, like the wild cat, is basically tabby in marking, and it is the artificial selection by breeders that has produced the wide array of self or solid colours as well as new patterns – from black, lilac and blue to tortoiseshell, smoke and many more.

Types of coat

The types of coat, like the colour, developed naturally in wild cats to suit the habitat. Desert-living types have shorter coats, while those dwelling in places with a more severe climate have much thicker ones.

The manul (*Felis manul*), for example, has a coat that is longer and denser than that of any other wild cat. It inhabits rocky mountainsides at heights up to 4,000 metres (13,000 feet) in Russian Asia, Tibet and Mongolia. This cat may possibly be the ancestor of longhaired domestic types, such as Angoras and blue, black, white and red longhairs (Persians).

Coats developed to suit different habitats

Longhair

Angora

American Wirehair

Maine Coon

Devon Rex

Cornish Rex

British or European Shorthair

Sphynx

There are three types of hair in a cat's coat:

- Guard hairs or topcoat
- Bristly awn hairs
- Soft and curly down hairs.

Hairs that are coloured are said to be tipped. The tipping may be light, or it may extend down the hair almost to the root. A ticked coat is one where the hairs carry bands of colour.

The particular mixture of the various hair types gives each breed its typical coat texture. Here are some examples:

- **Longhair** – a dense coat that has long guard hairs, up to 12.5 cm (5 in) and thick down hairs.
- **Angora** – very long guard and down hairs but finer and less profuse than in the Longhair.
- **Maine Coon** – long guard and down hairs (like the Longhair) but shaggy and uneven.
- **American Wirehair** – the coat has guard, awn and down hairs, all of which are curly, even coiled.
- **Cornish Rex** – the short and curly awn and down hairs are all of similar length.
- **Devon Rex** – the guard, down and awn hairs are all very short and curly.
- **Sphynx** – there are no guard or awn hairs, but a few down hairs on the face, tail and legs.

- **British or European Shorthair** – the guard hairs are about 4.5 cm (1³/₄ in) long, and the awn hairs are sparse.

Cats devote much of their day to grooming. Apart from keeping the coat clean and glossy, grooming removes dead hair and skin, tones muscles and stimulates blood circulation. This is one of the reasons why a mother cat cleans her kittens so frequently.

Nevertheless, self-grooming pets require additional help from their owners, particularly if they are Longhairs or Semi-Longhairs. A longhaired cat needs two 15–30-minute grooming sessions every day otherwise the coat will matt. The equipment needed comprises a wide, fine-toothed comb, a bristle and wire brush, a toothbrush (for cleaning the face), some bay rum conditioner (for dark cats) or talc (for light cats) and for show cats, a slicker brush to use on the tail.

Shorthaired coats are easier to manage. Two half-hour grooming sessions per week are ample. Grooming equipment includes a fine-toothed metal comb, a soft natural bristle brush or rubber brush. Bay rum conditioner can be used to remove grease from the coat and bring out the brilliance of its colour and a velvet, silk or chamois leather cloth is used for polishing.

Eyes

One of the most striking and attractive features of the cat is its eyes. The various breeds display a wide range of stunning colours and metal-like sheens by day and dramatic flashing and gleaming in the dark.

How do cats see in the dark?

The feline eye is constructed in much the same way as that of a human, but there are important modifications that enable the animal to do things we cannot.

Still basically a hunting animal, the domestic cat retains all the necessary perceptual abilities for the detection of prey that are used by the its wild forebears. A common belief is that cats can see in the dark. This is not, in fact, true. In a totally blacked-out room a cat can see no better than you or I could do. What it can do is gather the faintest quantities of light in its surroundings and enhance them. Even on a moonless night the sky is never completely devoid of light – faint starlight or the pale reflections of high clouds are always present – and the cat's eye is designed to gather and use such minute scraps of luminosity. We know that the domestic cat can make clear visual discrimination at one-sixth of the light levels required by human beings.

It uses an ingenious method in the form of a 'mirror' placed behind the light-sensitive retina. This 'mirror', the *tapetum lucidum*, is composed of up to 15 layers of glittering cells. Faint beams of light enter the eye and pass through it to hit and stimulate the light receptor cells of the retina. They then carry on past these cells and are reflected by the 'mirror' so that they make contact with the retina for as second time. This 'double dose' multiplies the effect of the light and immensely increases feline night vision.

The light receptor cells of the retina are of two types: the rods, which are sensitive to low light levels, and the cones, which provide resolving power. With the cat retina containing more rods and fewer cones than a human retina, cats see better than us in dim light but cannot discern fine detail quite as well as we can.

The shining of the *tapetum lucidum* is what produces the characteristic golden or green gleam of a cat's eye in the dark.

Some of the larger wild cats, such as pumas, have round pupils like humans. The

Cats display a wide range of eye colour

domestic cat, however, has a vertical slit pupil. The virtue of a slit pupil is that it can close more efficiently and completely than a round one, thereby protecting the ultra-sensitive retina.

Eye colours

The colour of a cat's eyes, which is controlled genetically, is contained within, and displayed by, the iris, which has pigment cells carrying particles of black, brown or yellowish hue. Where no pigment exists, as in albino cats, the iris is red-pink, all the colour coming from the blood vessels within.

Blue eyes are not caused by the presence of blue pigment but to the reflected light being 'scattered' from a faintly black-pigmented layer of the iris. Green eyes similarly possess no green pigment, but achieve their stunning effect by using scattered and reflected blue light, which then passes through a layer of yellowish pigment. The wide range of cat eye colours depends on the amount of pigment combined with the degree of light-scattering.

Some cat breeds may have eyes of various colours, while others present one colour only, albeit often in a range of shades. Blue-eyed breeds include the Snowshoe, Balinese, Birman and Ragdoll. The Havana,

Australian Mist, Kanaani, Chinchilla, Nebelung and some Singapuras have green eyes. You will see golden eyes in, among other breeds, the Chausie, Tiffany and some Chartreux.

Eye shapes

The shapes of cats' eyes are of three basic types:
- Round (as in Longhairs)
- Almond shaped
- Slanted

Sight

Cats possess a wider angle of view than humans. We have a visual field of around 210 degrees, of which 120 degrees is binocular. Cats have a total visual field of 285 degrees, 130 degrees of which is binocular. The 130-degree binocular vision of the cat is another hunting adaptation.

People sometimes wonder if their cat can see colours? Certainly the cones of their retinas are of at least two and possibly three kinds, and in humans cones certainly play a major part in colour vision. Scientists believe, however, that while cats can distinguish colours, it means nothing to them because their brains don't interpret them. Nevertheless, cats can, with difficulty, be trained to understand colour.

Slanted

Round/
Slanted

Almond

Round

Shorthairs

Shorthaired cats

Blue Shorthair

Short hair is much commoner than long hair in both wild and domestic cats. Genes that result in short hair are dominant over those that result in long hair. In the wild, long hair can cause problems when stalking and ambushing. It can get tangled on things and give enemies something to grab hold of. Without an attentive owner to do the grooming, it can become matted, leading perhaps to skin disease.

Coats with short hair are easier to care for – wounds can be tended without difficulty and, even though skin parasites can be a problem for shorthairs, they find a short coat an inconvenient environment in which to settle.

Types of shorthaired cats

Shorthaired cats have been around for thousands of years but pedigree breeds are a relatively new concept – they emerged with the first British cat shows held in the late 19th century. Shorthairs quickly became popular, as they are easy to maintain and also far less prone to hairballs in the stomach. There are three main categories of shorthaired cats, as detailled below.

British Shorthair

The British Shorthair is a sturdy cat with a strong, muscular body on short legs. It sports a short, dense coat, and the head is broad and rounded, with a short, straight nose and

American Shorthair

Siamese

large, round eyes. The European Shorthair breed is largely similar, but the body is not as cobby as that of the British equivalent.

American Shorthair

American Shorthairs developed from ancestors of the British and European Shorthairs, which were taken to North America by early settlers. These cats are larger and leaner than the British or European types, and have longer legs, more oblong heads with square muzzles, short, straight noses and large, round eyes.

Foreign or Oriental Shorthairs

The cats in this category have a quite different conformation from those of the British and American Shorthairs. They possess wedge-shaped heads with slanting eyes and large, pointed ears. They have lithe, slim bodies with long legs and fine, short coats. In some countries these cats are known simply as Oriental Shorthairs or as 'Oriental in type', whereas in other countries particular colours and coat patterns are designated as being either Foreign or Oriental.

Black Shorthair

Ideal cat-about-the-house

Size medium to large
Weight 2.5–6.5 kg (5^1/$_2$–14 lb)
Coat soft and dense
Lifespan 14+ years
Countries of origin various European countries

Eyes large and round; orange, gold or copper

Shorthaired black cats have been the object of fear, superstition and veneration down the ages, sometimes persecuted as creatures of ill omen, sometimes deified as bringers of good fortune.

This type of cat arose from the selective breeding of the best examples of street cats, and it was one of the first to be exhibited at London cat shows during the late 19th century.

The Black Shorthair has a short, dense, jet black coat without any white hairs. There is no undercoat. Too much basking in the sun can, however, induce a brownish tinge, an unwelcome feature in show specimens. The body is strong, stocky and muscular, and the cat has a round, broad head carrying a short, straight nose and medium-sized, round-tipped ears. In common with all the other Shorthair breeds, the eyes are large and round (non-pedigree shorthaired black cats usually have green eyes). The legs are short and well-proportioned and carry large, round paws, and the tail is short and thick.

This is a highly intelligent, easy-going and friendly cat that prefers an independent, outdoor life but does adjust to indoor living. It is a good mouser.

Minimal grooming is required.

White Shorthair
Streetwise and affectionate

Size medium to large
Weight 2.5–6.5 kg (5¹/₂–14 lb)
Coat soft and dense
Lifespan 14+ years
Countries of origin various European countries

Eyes large and round; blue, orange or odd (one orange, one blue)

In many countries white shorthaired cats are regarded as symbols of perfection and are greatly prized. Like the Black Shorthair, this breed's origins lie in the selective breeding of street cats in the late 19th century, and there are three varieties: Blue-eyed, Orange-eyed and Odd-eyed. As with black shorthaired cats, non-pedigree shorthaired white cats usually have green eyes.

The coat is short and dense, and pure, snowy white in colour without any tinge of grey or yellow. The cat has a strong, muscular and stocky body, a round, broad head with a well-developed chin and a straight nose, tipped by a pink nose pad. The medium-sized ears are set well apart and are round-tipped. The legs are short but well proportioned, and the large, round paws bear pink pads. The tail is short and thick.

As with other forms of white cat, the Blue-eyed variety is genetically predisposed to deafness. In Odd-eyed cats, which have one blue and one orange eye, deafness may be apparent only on the blue-eyed side. These cats are prone to sunburn and can develop skin carcinomas on their ear tips.

The White Shorthair is both intelligent and affectionate. Its short coat doesn't tend to tangle and merely requires a regular brush to remove dead hairs, to keep it looking glossy.

Cream Shorthair

Luscious looking and good natured

Size medium to large
Weight 2.5–6.5 kg (5¹/₂–14 lb)
Coat soft and dense
Lifespan 14+ years
Countries of origin various European countries

Eyes large and round; copper, orange or golden

The British or European Cream Shorthair is quite rare, and perfect examples are even rarer. It is now one of the most sought-after Shorthairs.

Cream Shorthairs originated towards the end of the 19th century when they started appearing accidentally in Tortoiseshell litters. By the 1920s breeding programmes had been established, although widespread interest did not become evident until the 1950s.

The coat of this cat is short, dense and fine, and the even-toned cream colour makes it look as if it has been dunked in a pail of clotted cream. Breeders prefer the paler shades for show animals, but it is not easy to produce cats with the desired pale, even coloration, and good examples are less often

seen than other types of Shorthair. Breeding from Tortoiseshells tends to produce too red a coat, and, because the dominant tabby gene is difficult to suppress, many kittens retain tabby markings into adulthood. Even if these eventually fade, extreme hot or cold weather may cause them to reappear.

The cat has a strong, stocky and muscular body. The head is round and broad, and the short nose is tipped by a pink nose pad. The eyes are set wide apart, and the medium-sized ears have round tips. The legs are short but well proportioned, and they carry large, round paws with pink pads. The tail is short, thick and tapering.

These cats are among the best natured of the Shorthairs. They are bright animals, which show great affection and loyalty towards their owners. The kittens are playful, but the adults are delightfully placid.

These cats, like the other Shorthair breeds, need access to outdoors and the freedom to roam. However, they require only minimal grooming in the form of regular, light brushing.

Blue Shorthair

Affectionate and peaceable

Size medium to large
Weight 2.5–6.5 kg (5 1/2–14 lb)
Coat extremely soft and dense
Lifespan 14+ years
Countries of origin various European countries

Eyes large and round; orange or copper

It has an ideal physique, extra-plush fur and heavenly blue-grey colour set off by glowing eyes. Like the Cream Shorthair, it was developed in the late 19th century in breeding programmes that used the very best street cats. By the 1940s the type had begun to deteriorate because of the scarcity of studs during the Second World War and unsuitable out-crosses. The introduction of Blue Longhairs into breeding lines resulted in some improvement, but the fur tended to be too long. It was not until the 1950s that selective breeding was able to restore the original Blue Shorthair type.

Some cat associations consider the Chartreux (see pages 104–5) to be a variety of the Blue Shorthair or even make no distinction between the two. In North America, however, the Chartreux is in a completely separate class, where a sturdier cat than the British Blue is required, with a higher proportion of grey in its coat and a less rounded face.

The fur of the Blue Shorthair is short and dense and medium to light blue in colour. These are strong cats, with muscular, rather stocky bodies. The round, broad head carries a short, straight nose tipped by a blue nose pad. The short, well-proportioned legs have large, round paws and blue paw pads. The tail is thick and tapers to a rounded tip.

This highly intelligent and especially loving character makes a first-class companion pet.

Blue-cream Shorthair

Alert and inquisitive

Size medium to large
Weight 2.5–6.5 kg (5^1/$_2$–14 lb)
Coat soft and dense
Lifespan 14+ years
Countries of origin various European countries

Eyes large and round; orange, rich gold or copper

As its name suggests, this cat is, essentially, a cross between Blue and Cream Shorthairs. A comparatively new breed, Australian and British standards call for a subtly toned coat with an intermingling of the two colours; the American Blue-cream, in contrast, has clearly defined patches. The breed was not recognized by British cat associations until the late 1950s, and the best examples of the British or European Blue-cream have very pale colouring. The coat is soft and dense, and the cream hairs tend to be finer than the blue ones, meaning that the cat may need extra grooming when it is moulting. Because of the way the colour genes are linked to sex in some cats, no male Blue-creams have been recorded as reaching adulthood.

These cats are powerfully built with muscular, stocky bodies. The broad, round head bears a short, straight nose with a blue nose pad and a well-developed chin. The medium-sized ears have round tips. The legs are short and well proportioned with large, round pads that are pink or blue or a mixture of the two colours. The tail is short and thick.

The Blue-cream has an inquisitive nature, and it loves to open drawers and cupboard doors, but its affectionate and lively temperament has endeared it to countless fond owners.

Tabby Shorthair
Loyal and affectionate

Size medium to large
Weight 2.5–6.5 kg (5¹/₂–14 lb)
Coat soft and dense
Lifespan 14+ years
Countries of origin various European countries

Colours shades of brown, black and cream (but no white)
Eyes large and round; gold, orange or copper or green or hazel

With its classic design and patterning the Tabby is the closest that the modern domestic cat comes to its pre-domestic ancestors. The tabby gene is a dominant one, and the newborn kittens of other breeds often have faint, transient, tabby markings that bear witness to their original ancestry. Tabby cats are depicted on the murals of the Egyptian Pharaohs, and in fact the word 'tabby' comes from Attabiya, a quarter of old Baghdad in which a striped cloth was made that was known in Europe as tabbi silk.

The modern, pedigree Tabby Shorthair originated, like other Shorthair breeds, in the 19th century through the crossing of the best of common-or-garden street cats.

There are two types of coat pattern: the Mackerel and the Classic. The Mackerel is more striped and lacks the spirals of the Classic. Classic Tabbies have a butterfly shape on the shoulder from which three stripes run along the spine, an oyster-shaped spiral on each flank and narrow, necklace-like stripes across the chest. The abdomen is spotted, and the forehead bears marks that form the letter M. The legs and tail are evenly ringed. The coat is short and plush and may be in one of several colours, including Red, Brown and Silver, and, in the USA, Blue and Cream.

The cats have the main physical characteristics of other Shorthair breeds. They are strong, stocky and muscular, with a

round, broad head, a short, straight nose and a well-developed chin. The eyes are copper, gold or orange in colour (or green or hazel in Silvers). The round-tipped ears are medium sized. The short, well-proportioned legs have large, round paws with deep red paw pads. The tail is short and thick.

This is a good-natured, affectionate and intelligent cat. The most popular variety, and the one that many claim to be the most friendly, is the Silver Classic Tabby Shorthair.

Tortoiseshell Shorthair

Sharp-witted, charming and friendly

Size medium to large
Weight 2.5–6.5 kg (5¹/₂–14 lb)
Coat soft and dense
Lifespan 14+ years
Countries of origin various European countries and USA

Colours shades of black, cream and red
Eyes large and round; deep orange or copper

The Tortie, as it is affectionately known, has been around for well over 100 years. When the earliest shows were held in the late 19th century, the Tortoiseshell was one of the first cats on the benches.

Like most British or European Shorthairs, the Tortoiseshell was developed by selective breeding of street cats, but it is, in fact, surprisingly difficult to breed. A virtually female-only breed, the Tortoiseshell is the centre of some debate on how to go about breeding it. American breeders do not regard it as especially problematic, whereas in Britain the desired mixture of red, cream and black patches has proved more elusive, with good specimens being quite rare. In recent years DNA testing of the cats has improved matters. To produce the desired patterning, queens are best mated with a solid-coloured black, cream or red stud, but even then the ensuing litter may contain only one kitten conforming to type.

There are two varieties to the breed. The Tortoiseshell-and-white Shorthair, once known as the Chintz or Spanish Cat, is exactly the same as the Tortie, but with added white

patches. In the fairly recently developed and very lovely Blue Tortoiseshell-and-white variety, the black and red in the coat of the Tortoiseshell-and-white is replaced by blue and cream. In the USA this cat is known as a Dilute Calico.

These cats have strong, muscular, stocky bodies. The round, broad head has a straight nose, large, round eyes and medium-sized ears with round tips. The short legs are well proportioned with large, round paws. The tail is short and thick.

Exceedingly good natured, the Tortie has long been one of the most popular companion cats.

Spotted Shorthair

Even-tempered and affable

Size medium to large
Weight 2.5–6.5 kg (5¹/2–14 lb)
Coat soft and dense
Lifespan 14+ years
Countries of origin various European countries

Colours silver-grey with black markings
Eyes large and round; green or hazel

The short, dense coat of this beautiful, eye-catching cat might well make it fall prey to cat thieves. Affectionately known as Spottie, this is basically a Mackerel Tabby with the markings broken up into spots.

A cat very similar to the Spotted Shorthair was known in Ancient Egypt, where it was revered as the killer of the serpent of evil. This Shorthair breed was also originally developed from street cats in the late 19th century, but it fell out of favour in the early 1900s, only regaining its popularity in the 1960s.

This breed is available in all the tabby-type colours with spots to match. In common with other Shorthair breeds, the cat has a strong, muscular body with a round, broad head, carrying a well-developed chin and a short, straight nose. The eyes are outlined in black, and the round-tipped ears are medium sized. The legs are short and well proportioned with large, round paws. The tail is short and thick.

The Spotted Shorthair is not only lovely to look at but also good natured and gentle.

Bi-colour Shorthair

Affectionate and intelligent

Size medium to large
Weight 2.5–6.5 kg (5^1/2–14 lb)
Coat soft and dense
Lifespan 14+ years
Countries of origin various European countries

Colours black and white, blue and white, cream and white or red and white
Eyes large and round; orange or copper

Pedigree specimens of this attractive breed are not easy to find because it is so difficult to meet the breed standards for patching of the coat. There are four varieties: Black-and-white (known as the Magpie), Blue-and-white, Red-and-white and Cream-and-white. The last of these, the Cream-and-white, is the most uncommon of the varieties. Kittens of all the varieties mature quite quickly.

A well-known forebear of Blue-and-white Bi-colour Shorthairs was a cat once owned by the Earl of Southampton, a friend of Shakespeare. A contemporary painting shows the earl and his cat imprisoned together in the Tower of London. The cat was said to have located his master's cell and then gained access by climbing down the chimney.

The physical build of the Bi-colour Shorthair is the same as for the Spotted Shorthair. Temperamentally, these are affectionate and intelligent cats.

Smoke Shorthair
Beguiling and affectionate

Size medium to large
Weight 2.5–6.5 kg (5¹/₂–14 lb)
Coat soft and dense
Lifespan 14+ years
Countries of origin various European countries

Colours black, tortoiseshell or blue over white
Eyes large and round; orange, copper or golden

The one-coloured topcoat is over a white undercoat, and when the cat is still it appears to be solid coloured. When it moves, however, the white can be seen flickering through the short, dense fur to produce a most glamorous, hazy effect.

The breed originated in the late 19th century from the crossing of Silver Tabbies with solid-coloured Shorthairs. Today, Smokes are usually mated to other Smokes or to Blue Shorthairs. There are three varieties of Smoke in Europe and the USA: the Black Smoke, the Tortie Smoke and the Blue Smoke.

The cats have strong, muscular bodies. The round, broad head carries a short, straight nose and medium-sized, round-tipped ears.

The short, well-proportioned legs have large, round paws, and the tail is short and thick.

The Smoke Shorthair is a good-natured, intelligent and most affectionate animal.

Tipped Shorthair

Irresistible and loyal

Size medium to large
Weight 2.5–6.5 kg (5¹/2–14 lb)
Coat soft and dense
Lifespan 14+ years
Countries of origin various European countries

Colours any Shorthair colour and chocolate or lilac over white
Eyes large and round; orange, copper or green

Another enchanting cat, the Tipped Shorthair has a tipped topcoat over a white undercoat, making a fascinating combination that produces a distinct sparkle as the cat moves.

The breed was created through a complex breeding programmes, involving Blues, Smokes and cats with silver genes. Known originally as a Chinchilla Shorthair, it was recognized under its present name in 1978.

There are several varieties. The tipping can be that of any British or European Shorthair colour, with the addition of chocolate and lilac. All varieties have orange or copper-coloured eyes, except the Black-tipped Shorthair, which has green eyes, outlined in black.

The physical appearance of the Tipped Shorthair is the same as that of the Smoke, and like those cats they are strong and muscular.

Good-humoured, intelligent and very loyal, the Tipped makes an affectionate and charming companion.

American Shorthair

Intelligent and hardy

Size medium to large
Weight 3–5.5 kg (6¹/₂–12 lb)
Coat thick, dense and hard
Lifespan 14+ years
Countries of origin Europe but developed in the USA after arriving with the Pilgrim Fathers

Colours most colours and patterns
Eyes large and wide with upper lid shaped like half an almond and lower lid a fully rounded curve; colour matches that of coat

This athletic cat is eminently adapted to the ethos of a country forged by frontiersmen and women. The modern American Shorthair was developed in the early 20th century by selective breeding from non-pedigree cats until they bred true to a type that stayed constant. A tough 'working cat', it is a fine controller of rodents but also makes a very good family pet.

The body of the American Shorthair is more powerful, sturdier and leaner than those of its British or European relations. It is particularly well balanced, with well-developed shoulders, chest and hindquarters.

The head is large and almost oblong in shape, but with full cheeks. The nose is of medium length, as are the round-tipped ears. The legs are heavily muscled and medium in length (slightly longer than those of the British or European Shorthairs), and they carry heavy, rounded paws. The tail is medium in length, tapering to a rounded tip.

This is an amenable and adaptable animal. Not prone to behavioural problems, it is good-natured and affectionate, and just as happy to spend time with its owner as it is out hunting in the garden or farmyard. Generally robust, the breed is a mostly healthy one.

American Wirehair

Interested in everything

Size medium to large
Weight 3.5–5 kg (8–11 lb)
Coat tightly crimped, thick, springy and coarse
Lifespan 14+ years
Country of origin USA

Colours all the colours and patterns of the American Shorthair
Eyes large, round and set well apart; brilliant gold in colour, but deep blue, odd-eyed, green and hazel are acceptable if complementing the coat colour

The most remarkable thing about this still fairly uncommon cat is its coat. The fur is unique among cats. Each of the guard hairs, the long, thick hairs of a cat's coat that are raised when the fur 'stands on end', is crimped along its length and hooked at the end. This results in a fur that is frizzy and wiry and, to the touch, not unlike the wool on a lamb's back. Even the whiskers are curly or wavy.

Although similar cats are recorded as having been found on London bomb sites after the end of the Second World War, the modern American Wirehair is descended from a shorthair queen living in New York in 1966, which gave birth to an unusual mutant red-and-white male with a wavy coat. Subsequently, breeding lines were established in the USA, Canada and Germany.

This is a cat with a medium-sized, well-muscled body, a round head with a well-developed muzzle and chin, a medium-length nose, medium-sized, round-tipped ears, medium-length, muscular legs bearing large, compact, oval paws and a medium-length tail tapering to a rounded tip. It is almost identical to the American Shorthair, except for the structure of its coat.

The American Wirehair has an even-tempered, affectionate nature. Somewhat

reserved and quiet, it purrs a lot. It is intelligent and active, loving to be out and about exploring and investigating things, and it makes a superb family pet.

Matings between American Wirehairs and American Shorthairs have produced a wide array of Wirehair varieties, of which the Patched Tabby is one of the more unusual. Such matings generally produce litters of 50 per cent Wirehairs.

Tonkinese

A people-oriented cat

Size medium
Weight 2.5–5 kg (5½–11 lb)
Coat medium-short, soft and close lying with a natural sheen; looks and feels like mink
Lifespan 14+ years
Country of origin USA

Colours solid, colourpointed, tortie and tabby, including brown, blue, chocolate, lilac, red, cream, caramel and apricot; in the USA mink shades include natural, champagne, blue, platinum and honey; the colours should shade to a slightly lighter tone on the underparts, with points that are clearly defined, but less distinct than those of a Siamese
Eyes medium in size, almond shaped and set wide apart; aquamarine to turquoise

Tonks, as they are affectionately known, were developed originally in the USA in the 1930s by crossing Siamese and Burmese, and they were then called Golden Siamese. Only in the late 1960s did they make their debut as the Tonkinese, named after the Gulf of Tonkin that lies between Myanmar (Burma) and Thailand (Siam).

This cat has a lithe and muscular body, midway in type between the svelte Siamese and the more compact Burmese. The wedge-shaped head has a long nose and square muzzle, the colour of the nose pad harmonizing with that of the coat. The ears are of medium size, broad at the base with oval tips. The legs are long, slim and elegant, ending in dainty oval feet. The tail, which is long in proportion to the body, is tapered.

There are several varieties with different coat colours and markings, including Natural Mink, Blue Mink, Honey Mink, Champagne Mink and, most glorious of all, Platinum Mink.

The Tonk is ultra-affectionate and loyal. It adores people and loves to be involved in

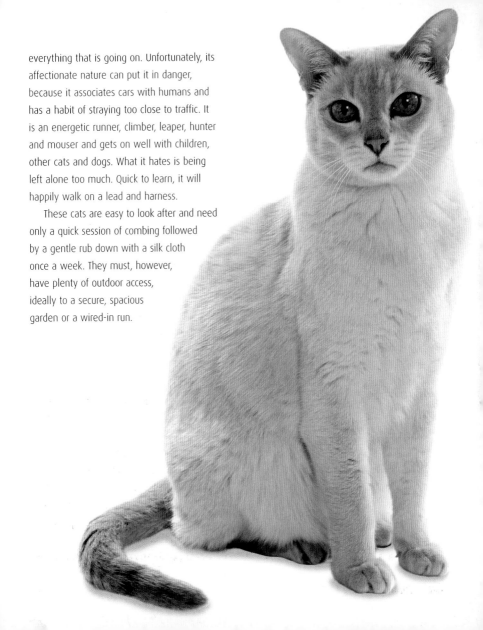

everything that is going on. Unfortunately, its
affectionate nature can put it in danger,
because it associates cars with humans and
has a habit of straying too close to traffic. It
is an energetic runner, climber, leaper, hunter
and mouser and gets on well with children,
other cats and dogs. What it hates is being
left alone too much. Quick to learn, it will
happily walk on a lead and harness.

These cats are easy to look after and need
only a quick session of combing followed
by a gentle rub down with a silk cloth
once a week. They must, however,
have plenty of outdoor access,
ideally to a secure, spacious
garden or a wired-in run.

Manx

The ideal family cat

Size medium
Weight 3.5–5.5 kg (8–12 lb)
Coat glossy, double type with a short, very thick undercoat and a slightly longer topcoat
Lifespan 12+ years
Country of origin Isle of Man (off the north-west coast of England)

Colours most recognized colours, colour combinations and coat patterns; some colours are not allowed by certain cat associations
Eyes large and round and set at a slight angle towards the nose; the colour should conform to the coat

This is the cat with no tail. Legend has it that the unfortunate Manx lost its tail when Noah closed the door to the ark a little too hastily, but in truth the real origins of the Manx are not known. Theories have included the possibility that tailless cats swam to the island from the English mainland, that they came with the shattered Spanish Armada in 1588 or that they arrived on merchant ships from the Far East. Whatever their origin, the isolation of the island allowed the tailless trait to be perpetuated.

A true or 'rumpy' Manx should have only a small hollow where a tail would have been. Cats with residual tails are also born, and depending on tail length these are known as Risers, Stumpies or Stubbies and Longies.

Unfortunately, the mutant gene responsible for the lack of tail is also implicated in defects in the cats' skeletal development. As a result, like-to-like matings of completely tailless Manx usually result in the kittens dying before, or shortly after, birth.

The Manx is a stocky cat with a strong, muscular body. The round, broad head has a short to medium length nose and medium-sized ears with slightly rounded tips. The forelegs are shorter than the hindlegs, with heavy, muscular thighs and large, round paws.

This cat has an excellent, placid, good-natured temperament. It emits a pleasant 'trilling' sound when talking to kittens or its owner. It is a good jumper and climber, and in its enthusiasm for chasing, retrieving and burying toys it is positively dog like.

Siamese

Importuning and arrogant

Also known as Wichien-maat (moon diamond)
Size medium
Weight 2–4.5 kg (4 1/2–10 lb)
Coat short, fine textured and glossy
Lifespan 14+ years
Country of origin Thailand (Siam) probably, but perhaps from some other Southeast Asian country

Colours pale (magnolia, ivory, off-white cream) with frosty-grey shading on the 'points' (mask, ears, legs and tail); the main four point colours and the only ones recognized by the breed societies in the USA are Seal, Blue, Lilac and Chocolate; other varieties are Red-point, Cream-point, Tabby-point, Seal Tortie-point, Blue Tortie-point, Chocolate Tortie-point and Lilac Tortie-point

Eyes medium in size and almond shaped; sapphire blue

These cats are known to have been kept as pets in the royal court of Siam (now Thailand) as early as the late 16th century, but a 14th-century book of cat poems depicts a Siamese-type cat called the *vichien mas*. Although it is often claimed that Siamese were first imported into Britain in the 1880s and into the USA not long afterwards, US President Rutherford B. Hayes is known to have received one, named Siam, as a gift from the US consul in Bangkok in 1878, six years before the first ones arrived in Britain.

The body is long, lithe, athletic and svelte in appearance. The long, slim legs end in dainty, oval feet, and a long, narrow, wedge-shaped head carries large, pointed ears. The tail is long, thin and tapering. Siamese kittens are born without points. The distinctive colouring develops gradually but it becomes distinct enough to recognize the cat's colour by the time the youngster reaches four weeks of age.

By nature Siamese can be demanding and often jealous or downright intolerant of any rivals in the household. The cat will make its feelings apparent by means of a distinctive, loud, low-pitched voice, which has been compared to the cries of a human baby – it is impossible to ignore. Nevertheless, this distinctly extrovert and highly intelligent cat loves company and is extremely affectionate. Give it plenty of attention, and it will become your loyal friend. A Siamese in the family will often bond strongly to a single person.

Like other blue-eyed white cats, Siamese can have some degree of reduced hearing ability, but the vast majority are not deaf. Indeed, they are an exception to the rule that white, blue-eyed cats are invariably deaf.

Russian Blue

Plushly independent

Also known as Archangel Cat,
Spanish Cat and Maltese Cat
Size medium
Weight 2.5–5.5 kg (5½–12 lb)
Coat short coat of the double type
that stands out from the cat's body
because of its density
Lifespan 14+ years
Country of origin Russia

Colours slate blue or pale blue with a distinct sheen produced by silver-tipped guard hairs;
White and Black varieties are recognized in some countries and are most popular in New Zealand
Eyes set wide apart and almond shaped in Britain but more rounded in the USA; vivid green

This handsome cat is a natural Russian breed, and Russian people consider it to be a welcome omen of good luck. Perhaps the most famous and most cosseted Russian Blue was Vashka, the pet of Tsar Nicholas I. Vashka had his own personal chef who prepared elaborate dishes containing such items as edible dormice and Sukhumi cheese.

The breed declined sharply during the Second World War, but concerted efforts by breeders in Europe and the USA led to its revival in the late 1960s.

Russian Blues have long, slender, elegant bodies and long, fine-boned legs. The short, wedge-shaped head bears a medium long nose and large, slightly pointed and almost transparent ears. There is a long, slender neck and a long tail tapering from a moderately thick base. The paws are small and oval with blue pads in Europe and more rounded with pink or mauve pads in the USA.

The cat has a sweet-natured, quiet and reserved character. In fact, queens can be so quiet that it may be difficult to tell when they are calling in oestrus. Russian Blues don't tend to go wandering, apparently preferring the indoor life. They get on well with children, other cats and dogs, but they do not like excessive handling or being teased. Loving and loyal, they make excellent indoor pets and are, at the same time, one of the few breeds that are amenable to being trained to walk on a lead.

Abyssinian

Attentive and intelligent

Size medium
Weight 3–5.5 kg (6¹/₂–12 lb)
Coat glossy and soft but also dense
and resilient to the touch
Lifespan 14+ years
Country of origin not known for
certain but possibly Egypt

Colours ticked coat in Usual (ruddy brown), Sorrel, Blue, Fawn, Lilac, Silver Sorrel, Silver Blue,
Tortoiseshell, Chocolate, Red and Cream colours
Eyes large and almond shaped; amber, hazel or green

The origins of this handsome, rather wild-looking cat are not recorded, and it is probably a very old, natural breed. Modern Abyssinians may be descended from a female called Zula, which was imported into Britain from Ethiopia in 1868, but some breeders point out that the Romans are known to have imported cats from Egypt into Britain and may thereby have introduced the 'Egyptian look' into the native feline population. Whatever the truth, many Abyssinian enthusiasts believe that the cats are direct descendants of the sacred cats of the pharaohs.

The Abyssinian has a medium length, lithe, graceful and muscular body. The round, gently wedge-shaped head carries a medium-sized nose and large, pointed and tufted ears, which are set well apart. The long, slender, fine-boned legs, which give the impression that the cat is on tip-toe when it is standing, end in small, oval paws. The fairly long, tapering tail is thick at the base.

This is a sweet-tempered, affectionate, obedient and highly intelligent cat. Alert and lively, it loves to play and much prefers being outdoors to in. The Abyssinian needs lots of fuss and attention to keep it happy. It dislikes

being confined and pines if deprived of human company. Overall, it makes a fine family pet, but it is not a suitable cat for an elderly person living alone and wanting an indoor companion.

Korat

Good-looking and good with children

Also known as Si-sawat, Cloud-coloured Cat, Blue Cat of Thailand, Koraj and Good-luck Cat

Size medium
Weight 2.5–5 kg (5¹/₂–11 lb)
Coat sleek and glossy without an undercoat
Lifespan 12+ years
Country of origin Thailand

Colours blue-grey with silver-tipped guard hairs creating an attractive sheen
Eyes brilliant green sometimes with a tinge of amber; kittens may have amber eyes that turn green later

One of the oldest natural breeds, the Korat is said to have been named after the Thai province where it originated by King Rama V. In Thailand it is known as Si-sawat, which refers to the good fortune that its possession is believed to bring. The first Korat to be officially exhibited in Europe was entered in a British cat show in 1896 – as a blue Siamese – and the first pair of these cats was imported into the USA as recently as 1959.

The cat's most striking features are the prominent, round and luminous green (peridot) eyes and the wonderful short, fine and silky coat of silver-blue, which has a distinct sheen. An ancient book of cat poems held in the Bangkok National Library describes the Korat thus: 'The hairs are smooth, with tips like clouds and roots like silver; the eyes shine like dewdrops on a lotus leaf.' Korat kittens often have amber-coloured eyes, which steadily turn green as they grow older.

The body is semi-cobby, lithe and muscular. The heart-shaped head carries

large, high-set, round-tipped ears. The legs are slim and of medium length, with the forelegs being slightly shorter than the hindlegs, and the paws are small and oval with dark blue to pinkish-lavender-coloured pads. The tail is of medium length and has a round tip. A characteristic feature of this cat's coat is the way the fur breaks when the back is bent. The absence of a full undercoat can result in Korats being rather susceptible to chills in colder climates.

Beautiful, intelligent, playful and good natured, the Korat makes an ideal pet, particularly for children. It also tends to be talkative when spoken to and is intensely loyal.

Havana

Active, affectionate and intelligent

Also known as Havana Brown
Size medium
Weight 3–4 kg (6½–9 lb)
Coat short and glossy
Lifespan 14+ years
Countries of origin Britain and USA

Colours rich chestnut-brown
Eyes almond shaped and slanted; pale to mid-green

The only connection that this breed has with the island of Cuba is that its luxurious coat is the colour of expensive cigar tobacco. The Havana originated in Britain in the 1950s from the crossing of a Seal-point Siamese with a black shorthaired cat of Siamese ancestry. The British breeding programme continued to use Siamese out-crosses, but US breeders decided not to use Siamese blood, preferring to produce a cat that was less Oriental in type and whose looks more closely resembled those of the original imports.

The British Havana is a long, svelte, muscular, Siamese-type animal, with a long, wedge-shaped head and short, straight nose and large, slightly pointed ears. It has long, slim legs with the forelegs shorter than the hindlegs, small oval paws, and a long, elegant tail.

The American Havana is a sturdier cat with a medium-length torso, rounder face, oval eyes, round-tipped ears and longer fur. Its physique is closer to that of a Russian Blue than a Siamese. There is one colour variety, the Frost, which is exclusive to the USA.

Havanas are loyal and loving, but they demand company and plenty of attention. To be contented, they need a lot of mental stimulation for they are both spirited and highly inquisitive – watch your drawers and refrigerator doors. In addition, they love

being stroked and cuddled. The American
Havana tends to be somewhat quieter than its
British cousin.

The Havana hates to be left at home
alone, so it should be provided with another
cat to keep it company in households where
its owners go out to work.

Burmese

Fun-loving with a big personality

Size small to medium
Weight 3.5–5.5 kg (8–12 lb)
Coat glossy, short and with a satin finish
Lifespan 14+ years
Country of origin Burma (Myanmar)

Colours Brown, Blue, Chocolate, Lilac, Red and Cream; Tortie colours are the same except for Red and Cream
Eyes lower lids rounder than upper lids, giving a slanted appearance; any shade of yellow to gold

Brown cats similar to today's Burmese, known as Rajahs, were recorded as dwelling in Buddhist temples in Burma in the 15th century. The modern breed was founded by Wong Mau, a cat imported into the USA from Burma in 1930, which was crossed with a Siamese tom. There may have been subsequent imports of cats from Burma, but by 1936 the cats were breeding true enough to be granted recognition by the US cat fancies. In the 1940s the large amount of Siamese blood that had been introduced caused the original type to be overwhelmed and recognition was temporarily suspended. The breed was once again recognized in the USA in 1953, just after it received British recognition for the first time.

The number of varieties of Burmese differs in Britain and the USA, and the American Burmese has a rounder body, head, eyes and feet than the British cat.

The Burmese has a more muscular and rounded body than the Siamese, with a medium, wedge-shaped head with a fairly short nose and medium-sized ears set well apart and slightly rounded at the tips. The legs are long and slim with small, oval paws, whose pads conform to the colour of the coat. The medium-length tail is straight, tapering only very close to the rounded tip.

These intelligent and highly affectionate cats love people, and they make superb pets. However, they can be quite demanding, pestering to get what they want, and they don't like being teased.

Burmese cats do tend to be fascinated by wool and other materials. They will lick and chew it and sometimes swallow it, with consequent problems developing in the stomach and intestines.

Asian Self

Beautiful, fun-loving and affectionate

Also known as European Burmese
Size small to medium
Weight 4–5.5 kg (9–12 lb)
Coat smooth and close lying
Lifespan 12+ years
Countries of origin Britain, USA and
other countries worldwide

Colours Brown, Blue, Chocolate, Lilac, Red and Cream; Tortie colours are the same except for
Red and Cream
Eyes rounded, slightly slanted, full and expressive and set well apart; colour complements coat
colour, but mainly gold, yellow or green

These charming cats with their sleek and
shiny coats are the epitome of Oriental
elegance. They originated from the Burmese
breed and a range of out-crossings.
Physically, they are of medium build, and
females are much smaller and daintier than
males. They have a strong, muscular body
with a straight back. The head is short and
round with a gently rounded dome and a
short nose and muzzle. The ears are medium
sized to large, round tipped, set well apart
and tilted slightly forwards. The legs are of
medium length, with the hindlegs a little

longer than the forelegs. The paws are oval
in shape, and the tail is medium to long,
tapering to a rounded tip.

Varieties of the breed are the Asian
Smoke (once called the Burmoire) and the
Black Asian Self, also known as the Bombay
(see pages 86–7). The Burmilla (see pages
92–3) and Tiffany (see pages 158–9) are
basically the same as the Asian Self.

This cat is loving and loyal, much like the
Burmese but a little less boisterous. It adores
being part of the family and can be quite
demanding, following an owner around the

house and crying for attention. Inquisitive and intelligent, the Asian Self is adept at working out how to open doors and cupboards. It loves to play and gets on well with children, other cats and dogs.

Fond of home comforts, this cat is happy to live a largely indoor life, but it must be provided with toys to keep it amused, and it demands plenty of quality time and attention from its owners. The Asian Self can be trained to walk on a lead, as long as the process is begun when the cat is young. The cat requires minimal grooming, but it will relish the attention when it is combed.

Savannah

Highly intelligent and playful

Size large
Weight 4.5–9 kg (10–20 lb)
Coat somewhat coarse and close lying
Lifespan 12+ years
Country of origin USA

Colours Black, Black Smoke, Brown Spotted Tabby and Silver Spotted Tabby; the colour markings often resemble those of the serval
Eyes 'boomerang' shaped with a slightly hooded brow; blue in kittens, but yellow, gold, green or caramel-brown in adults

In the mid-1980s a domestic shorthair was crossed with a serval, the wild cat with long legs, slim build and large, oval ears that is widely distributed throughout sub-Saharan Africa. Later generations involved out-crossings with Oriental Shorthairs, Egyptian Maus, Serengetis, Bengals and non-pedigree cats.

The Savannah is a long, leggy cat that, when standing, is higher at the hind end than at the shoulders. Its tall, slim build gives it the appearance of greater size than its actual weight. The head is an elongated wedge set on a long, slender neck. The tall, erect ears have central light-coloured bands bordered by black on the posterior surface, and the tail is short with black rings and a most attractive black tip.

This is a highly intelligent breed, expert at jumping – up to 2.4 metres (8 feet) from a standing position – most inquisitive and quick to learn how to open doors and drawers. They are fascinated by water, playing in it and even going under the shower with their owners.

The Savannah is quite vocal and has a range of 'voices', chirping like a serval, mewing like a domestic cat or emitting a rather dramatic and loud hiss, which is more like the sound of an enraged snake than the noise usually made by a cross domestic cat.

Temperamentally, the breed is sociable, friendly and almost dog like in its loyalty to its owner, although some individuals are suspicious of strangers. The cat will follow its owner around the house and can readily be taught to walk on a lead and to retrieve objects. It likes to be involved in family life.

Savannahs make good family pets as long as they have plenty of secure space indoors and outside, where they can romp and play with a variety of playthings, and they must receive plenty of attention, affection and interaction from family members. They are not suitable for an elderly person living alone who wants an armchair companion.

Singapura

Rare but a great indoor pet

*Also known as Kucinta, Drain Cat
and River Cat*
Size small to medium
Weight 2–4 kg (4$^{1}/_{2}$–9 lb)
Coat short, silky and close lying
Lifespan 12+ years
Country of origin possibly Singapore
or may have been produced
'artificially' in the USA

Colours Sepia Agouti, which is old (gold) ivory, with bands of dark bronze and warm cream ticking
Eyes large, almond shaped and slanted; hazel, green or yellow

It is not certain whether the Singapura is a true native of the island of Singapore (Singapura is the Malaysian name for Singapore) or a cat that was created by crossing Burmese and/or Abyssinians in the USA. Cats similar to the Singapura are numerous throughout Southeast Asia, not just in Singapore. Certainly an American couple brought them into the United States in 1975. The breed arrived in Britain in 1989.

The cat has a muscular, moderately stocky body, a rounded head with a short nose and large slightly pointed ears. The medium-length muscular legs end in small oval paws with rosy brown pads, and there is a fairly short, slender tail.

The unfortunate name Drain Cat arose because, in its native land, the Singapura appears to seek shelter and a place to nap in drains.

The breed hates cold, wet weather. It enjoys playing and climbing – its predilection for perching on high places allows it a better view of its surroundings – and it never quite stops being a kitten. It is somewhat shy and reserved but is nonetheless a social cat that adores human company, and as such it makes a perfect indoor companion pet.

The only genetic-based health problem of Singapuras is the condition known as uterine inertia, when a queen is unable to give birth because of weakness in the muscles of the uterine wall. Individuals with uterine inertia may have to undergo Caesarian sections in order to deliver the foetus or foetuses. Pregnant cats need a pre-natal exam by a vet.

Bombay

A remarkable coat and a constant purr

*Also known as Black Asian Self and
Black Burmese*
Size Small to medium
Weight 3.5–5.5 kg (8–12 lb)
Coat gorgeous and ultra-smooth with
a sheen like patent leather
Lifespan 14+ years
Country of origin USA

Colour jet black
Eyes golden, vivid copper or yellow-green

This most elegant of cats gets its name from
the Indian city of Bombay (Mumbai) because
of its resemblance to the Indian black
leopard. The breed originated in Kentucky,
USA, in the 1950s by crossing a Burmese and
an American Black Shorthair, and then later,
in the 1960s, in Britain from accidental
matings of Burmese and non-pedigree
shorthairs. It is still fairly rare outside the USA.

Surprisingly heavy for its size, the
Bombay has a muscular body, medium-
length legs and small oval paws with black
pads. The tail is of medium length. The
rounded head has a full face tapering to a
short muzzle. The eyes are round and set far
apart, the ears are broad at the base with
gently rounded tips, and the nose pad is black.

The Bombay is smart and loyal and
makes a perfect pet. It rarely stops purring
and when pleased purrs loudly enough to be
heard in the next room. It craves human
companionship, hating to be left alone, and is
very happy to spend its entire life indoors,
seldom showing much interest in the great
outdoors. A quintessential lap cat, it adores
being petted and cuddled and is a confirmed
head bumper and nose rubber. This is an
intelligent, inquisitive breed that loves to

inspect anything or anybody newly arrived in the house. They are often chatty cats and have a distinctive voice. Bombays tend to adapt more quickly to living with dogs in the family than with other cats, which they usually want to dominate, and they are easy to look after, not needing much grooming or any special form of attention. As Bombays are very keen on stropping their claws, it is wise to install a scratching post for them to use to help save wear and tear on your furniture.

Snowshoe

Home-loving and adorable

Also known as Silver Laces
Size medium to large
Weight 2.5–5.5 kg (6–12 lb)
Coat short, glossy and medium-coarse
in texture
Lifespan 14+ years
Country of origin USA

Colours Blue, Sealpoint, Lilac and Chocolate; there are two colour patterns, both with the white paws of a Birman: the Mitted carries the Siamese (Himalayan) pattern with up to one-third of the body white, excluding the face, whereas the Bi-colour has up to two-thirds of the body white, including the face
Eyes large, slanting and oval: bright blue

This cat combines the beauty of the Siamese with the bulk of the American Shorthair. It originated in the 1960s when three kittens of Siamese parentage were born. American Shorthair bloodlines were introduced into them when they matured.

The graceful Snowshoe has a lithe, well-muscled body. The rounded, triangular-shaped head carries a medium-length nose, which is straight in profile, and large, pointed ears set well apart. The medium-length legs have medium-sized, oval paws with pink and grey pads. The medium-length tail tapers. The Snowshoe's name and nickname derive from the distinctive white paws. In many ways the breed's appearance resembles that of the Siamese of 50 years ago. and it does indeed look rather like a heavily built, more rounded Siamese. It is still a relatively rare breed.

The Snowshoe has been described as having a sparkling and imperturbable personality. It is lively, active and athletic, delighting in running, leaping and chasing toys, and it particularly relishes interactive games with its owners. An intelligent cat, it quickly learns how to open doors and can be taught tricks, especially retrieving. Most Snowshoes enjoy being around water and may even go swimming on occasion. Unusually, Snowshoes like being given a bath.

It prefers to have company most of the time, loves being petted and is excellent with children, other cats and dogs. It is more easy-going and less noisy than the Siamese, and it makes an ideal indoor pet, although it must have lots of attention. It also needs space and facilities to enable it to expend its boundless energy. It does not appreciate being left alone for long periods of time, and in households where family members are out at work all day it is best to have another cat to keep it company. The breed is particularly popular in the USA.

Oriental Shorthair

Chatty, athletic and affectionate

Size medium
Weight 3–4 kg (6¹/₂–9 lb)
Coat fine and glossy
Lifespan 12+ years
Countries of origin various, including
Britain and the USA

Colours the full range in Selfs, Torties, Smokes and Shadeds
Eyes green but blue in Whites; green also allowed in US Whites

The term 'Oriental' does not necessarily indicate an exotic origin for these cats, although some do, indeed, come from the Far East. Rather, it refers to a number of breeds that have a similar appearance. Foreign or Oriental Shorthairs have a conformation that is quite different from that of the British or European and American Shorthairs. They have a lithe, slim body with a wedge-shaped head, slanting eyes, large, pointed ears, long legs and a fine, short coat. The category includes some well-known breeds, including the Siamese (see pages 68–9), Korat (see pages 74–5) and Havana (see pages 76–7). One breed of Oriental Shorthair, the Seychellois, was an experimental Van-type patterned cat in both short and semi-longhair varieties, developed in the 1980's in the USA. Within twenty years however, it had disappeared.

There are differences between the British and US nomenclature for these cats. For example, the American Self Brown that followed the British Havana breeding programme is called the Oriental Self Brown, and the cats known as Oriental Whites in Britain are called American Foreign Whites in the USA.

Physically, the Oriental Shorthair is streamlined and heavier than it looks, with a very muscular frame. Its long, svelte body is carried on long, finely shaped legs.

The Oriental Shorthair has a superb temperament. It is loving and loyal, though perhaps a bit demanding, and it adores being fussed over and cuddled. Active and playful, it needs plenty of mental stimulation to keep it contented, particularly in the form of interaction with humans. It does not like being left alone, so working owners would be wise to have two cats, so that they can keep each other company and out of mischief.

Burmilla

Excellent, even-tempered disposition

Also known as Asian Shaded
Size medium
Weight 3.5–4.5 kg (8–10 lb)
Coat short (but longer than the Burmese) and soft and dense in texture
Lifespan 14+ years
Country of origin Britain

Colours Agouti (shaded) tipped with colours seen in Asian Selfs and Torties; the undercoat is white in Silver varieties and golden in non-Silvers
Eyes large and set well apart with a round lower lid and straight upper lid; yellow to green in colour and outlined in black or brown

In 1981 an accidental mating between a Lilac Burmese queen and a Chinchilla tom, both owned by Baroness Miranda von Kirchberg, produced four kittens, the Burmilla's founder members. They were of the Burmese type but had black-tipped silver coats. Today Burmillas still have the body conformation of a Burmese but with a softer, shaded or tipped coat.

The Burmilla's body is medium in length and lithe but muscular. The head is gently rounded and bears a short nose and a terracotta nose pad outlined in brown or black. The ears are medium to large, set well apart, broad at the base, have rounded tips and tilt slightly forwards. The legs are slim and of medium length, and the forelegs are slightly shorter than the hindlegs. The paws are a neat oval in shape, and the tail is medium to long, elegantly plumed and tapering to a round tip. It is ringed in the same colour as the tipping. Females are much smaller and daintier than males.

This is one of the gentlest, most loving and most even-tempered cats. Although less boisterous than the Burmese and not as easy-going as the Chinchilla, it loves to play, asks for plenty of attention, and is guaranteed to make a loyal and devoted companion. Burmillas do not have any specific health problems and do not tend to become obese through overeating. A word of caution: these cats are so friendly that they will happily wander around and approach strangers if they are left unattended outdoors. Because of this, many Burmillas have become lost or, worse, been stolen.

Devon Rex

A superb family cat

Also known as Butterfly Rex
Size small to medium
Weight 2-4.5 kg (4¹/₂-10 lb)
Coat short, fine, wavy and soft
though slightly coarser than that of
the Cornish Rex
Lifespan 14+ years
Country of origin Britain

Colours any
Eyes large, oval and set wide apart; any colour

In 1966 a curly-coated kitten was born to a non-pedigree queen that had been mated with a stray curly-coated tom. This kitten, a male named Kirlee, was then mated with Cornish Rex females, but only straight-coated litters were produced, and it was necessary to arrange inbreeding before the curly fur reappeared. At first it was believed that Cornish and Devon Rex cats were related, but we now know that their characteristic coats are caused by distinctly different genes.

The Devon Rex has a slender, hard, muscular body, a modified wedge-shaped head with full cheeks and a short nose, which creates an appearance that has been described as elfin or pixie like. It has long, slim legs with small oval paws. The long, fine, tapering tail is well covered in fur. The curly whiskers tend to be brittle.

This cat has the charming habit of wagging its tail like a dog when it is happy, a characteristic that has earned it the nickname 'poodle cat'.

Affectionate, active and playful, this cat is often rather mischievous, loving to leap, climb and play with toys, and it is expert at seeking out the warmest spots in the house for a nap or to rest. The Devon Rex is a home-loving

family cat, which is good with children, other cats and dogs, but it does expect – indeed, demands – a lot of attention from its owner. Because it does not shed much hair, it requires minimal grooming. However, because it has such a short coat it needs to live and sleep in a warm environment, and because it has a faster metabolism than other breeds, which is the result of its higher body temperature and consequent need for plenty of calories, it has a big, big appetite.

Cornish Rex

Naughty and inquisitive

*Also known as English Rex, Coodle,
British Cornish Rex and European
Cornish Rex*

Size small to medium
Weight 2–4 kg (4¹/₂–9 lb)
Coat wavy and silky
Lifespan 13+ years
Country of origin Britain

Colours any colours and markings
Eyes large and oval; any colour

Looking as if it has just returned from a visit to the hairdresser with a rather old-fashioned permanent wave, the Cornish Rex is named after the Rex rabbit, which also has a curly coat. Although Rex-type cats are pictured on postcards in Britain in the 19th century and were recorded in Germany in the early 1930s, the breed was not taken seriously until 1950, when a litter of farm kittens in Cornwall was found to contain a lovely cream male with wavy fur. It was mated back to its mother and found to breed true. A pregnant queen was exported to the USA in the late 1950s and established the breed there.

The body of the Cornish Rex is long, slender and muscular, and the cat has a naturally arched back. The wedge-shaped head has a long nose and large, slightly rounded, high-set ears. The cat stands high on its very long, straight and slender legs, which end in dainty, slightly oval paws. The highly flexible tail is long and slender and tapers towards the end. All coat colours and patterns, apart from bi-coloured, are recognized, and the eyes can be any colour but should harmonize with the coat.

The Cornish Rex is an affectionate and playful cat, and it loves being cuddled. It is

loyal and home-loving and is good with children, other cats and dogs. Nimble, lively and energetic, the cat is inquisitive and proficient at opening cupboard doors. The breed is generally quite vocal, and it loves warm nooks and corners.

Like other Rex breeds, the Cornish should have two half-hour grooming sessions per week using a rubber brush, which will not scratch the skin. The brush should be drawn along the lie of the hair.

German Rex
Affectionate, sociable and family-loving

Size small to medium
Weight 3–5 kg (6¹/₂–11 lb)
Coat curly; thicker than that of the Cornish Rex
Lifespan 14+ years
Country of origin Germany

Colours all colours
Eyes all colours

Although an earlier Rex-type cat is recorded as living in the early 1930s in Königsberg (now Kaliningrad), this breed probably originated in Germany in the 1950s when a Berlin doctor, Rose Scheuer-Karpin, came across a curly-haired cat in the grounds of the hospital where she was working. She named it Laemmchen (little lamb). Hospital staff told her that it had been around for at least four years, and it's interesting to note that Laemmchen eventually turned out to have belonged to a male nurse who arrived in Berlin in 1945 from Königsberg. The doctor assumed, almost certainly correctly, that Laemmchen was a spontaneous mutant, and so the 'little lamb' became the founding female of all German Rex cats. The breed nearly died out in 1999, but happily breeders in Germany, Finland, Switzerland, Russia, Holland and Denmark got together to re-establish a breeding programme, which is now flourishing.

This cat is of medium size with slender, medium-length legs. The head is round with large, open ears. The whiskers curl, though less than those of the Cornish Rex, and they may, in some individuals, be almost straight.

The German Rex is loving and quickly bonds with its owner. Intelligent, active and playful, it loves to climb, run and leap, and it will happily perform its acrobatic tricks time and time again. It is loyal and home loving and has a penchant for being cuddled – often. It is also very good with children, dogs, and other cats.

Selkirk Rex

Companionable but needs lots of grooming

Size medium to large
Weight 3–5.5 kg (6½–12 lb)
Coat curly, soft and dense
Lifespan 12+ years
Country of origin USA

Colours any
Eyes large and round; any colour

The breed was founded in 1987 by, Jeri Newman, a cat breeder in Montana. She began with a curly-coated, shorthaired, non-pedigree, rescued female, which she named Miss DePesto, apparently because the cat was always 'pestering' her for something, and a Black Persian tom. Later, she introduced blood lines from Persians, British Shorthairs and Exotic Shorthairs. The breed is quite distinct from other Rex breeds and has hair of normal length, with both longhaired and shorthaired varieties. The tightness of the coat curls or ringlets varies according to coat length, but they are generally loose and wavy.

This is a sturdy, solidly built, heavy-boned cat with the cobby build of a Persian. It has a round head with medium-sized ears, curly whiskers and eyebrows and a prominent muzzle. Semi-longhair varieties sport plumy tails and ruffs. The dense coat, which has a delightfully plush, 'teddy-bear' feel to it, tends to shed a lot and therefore requires regular and thorough grooming. In the mid-1980s American breeders developed the so-called Missouri Rex from crossing non-pedigrees and Devon Rex types. On testing it was found to be carrying the same 'curly' gene as the Selkirk Rex.

Selkirk Rex cats have excellent temperaments, being patient and tolerant, loving and loyal. They get on well with children, other cats and dogs, and they love to play games.

In general the breed is healthy and hardy and is not susceptible to any specific health problems. As with other Rex breeds, however, the curly fur can irritate the outer ear canal and, as a result, increase the production of ear wax. Owners need to inspect and, if necessary, clean their cat's ears at regular intervals.

Egyptian Mau

August and affectionate

Size medium
Weight 2.5–5 kg (5¹/2–11 lb)
Coat fine and silky but dense and resilient to the touch; the medium-length hairs carry two or more even bands of ticking
Lifespan 14+ years
Countries of origin Egypt and USA (the modern form)

Colours Silver, Bronze, Pewter, Smoke, Blue and Black; all but the Black have brown or black markings
Eyes pale 'gooseberry' green

Mau or Miw was the ancient Egyptian name for the cat that was worshipped as a god and, when it died, was mummified and buried in special cat cemeteries. The modern breed first appeared in Europe and the USA in the 1950s, cats having been imported from Cairo.

The Mau has a muscular body. The medium-length legs end in small, slightly oval feet, and the hindlegs are longer than the forelegs. The rounded, wedge-shaped head has a short nose and large, slightly pointed ears, and the tail is of medium length. Curiously, it carries on its forehead a pattern resembling the sacred scarab beetle, which is often found on the foreheads of cats depicted on Egyptian murals. No wonder many people believe that the Mau is descended from the cat symbolized by the ancient Egyptian gods of Ra and Bast that were worshipped by the pharaohs.

The Mau is the only naturally spotted breed of domestic cat, and it is also said to be the fastest runner.

The cat is naturally loving and playful. It is quite vocal and has a musical voice, cheeping, chuckling or squeaking when it is stimulated. When in a happy mood a Mau will commonly perform what is called the 'wiggle-tail' – that is, the cat, male or female, will move its back legs up and down, marching on the spot, as if marking territory by spraying but without actually releasing any urine. These cats adore being fussed over, and they make first-class family pets. It is one of the few breeds that enjoys going out for walks on a lead.

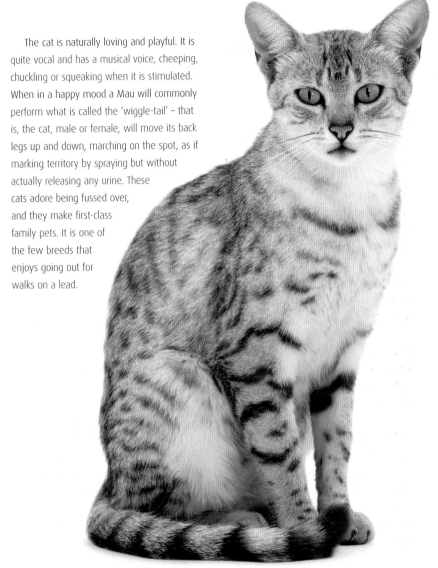

Chartreux

Sharp-witted and affectionate

Also known as Chartreuse, Certosino, Karthhauser, Karthuizer and French Cat
Size medium to large
Weight 3–5.5 kg (6½–12 lb)
Coat short and dense
Lifespan 15+ years
Country of origin France

Colours blue with silver highlights
Eyes large and round; gold, copper or brilliant orange

This is an old natural breed that is believed to have originated in the Middle Ages as companions to the monks of La Grande Chartreuse.

These cats have strong, muscular, stocky bodies with a round, broad head and a short, straight nose. The ears are medium sized and have round tips. The short but well-proportioned legs carry large, round pads. The tail is shortish and thick.

This breed is renowned for its beautiful grey-blue double coat, which is soft and lush and requires little grooming. Chartreux are slow-maturing cats: males achieve their maximum weight at four or five years of age, and females reach full size at around three years.

These are incredibly attentive, gentle and adaptable cats, and are dog-like in their devotion to owners. They are excellent with children, other cats, dogs and strangers. Intelligent animals, they quickly learn their names and come running when called. They are also quite agile and athletic and love playing games. Although comparatively large cats, they are quiet animals with a tiny voice and a sweet, smiling expression. Many are completely mute – they purr but cannot meow – while others occasionally emit a gentle, high-pitched miaow or chirp.

Bengal

Playful and talkative

Size medium to large
Weight 4.5–9 kg (10–20 lb)
Coat short to medium-length silky,
soft and thick fur
Lifespan 14+ years
Country of origin USA

Colours in Britain Brown (Black), both Spotted and Marbled, and Snow, both Spotted and
Marbled; in the USA Leopard (black spots on orange background), Mink (black spots on
mahogany background) and Sorrel (brown spots on light orange background)
Eyes large and round; gold, green or hazel in colour; blue or blue-green in Snows

This expensive cat originated in the USA from crossing a wild Asian leopard cat with a domestic Tabby, and many descendants of the first Bengals still retain distinctly wild instincts and are somewhat wild-looking.

The body is long, sleek and muscular. The large head bears a short nose and small to medium-sized ears. The legs are relatively short, and the hindlegs are somewhat shorter than the forelegs, which gives a 'stalking' appearance when the cat is walking. The paws are very large and round, and the tail is long and muscular. Overall the Bengal presents a highly athletic appearance.

When they are born Bengal kittens are spotted, but the initially rough fur disguises the patterning for the first three or four months in the majority of cases.

This is a highly resourceful, confident, self-possessed and intelligent breed. Like its wild relative, it thrives in an environment that is physically and mentally stimulating. It is attracted to water and likes playing with it, and it is a keen collector of frogs and toads, which it delights in bringing home as presents for its owner.

The Bengal is playful, chatty and sociable, enjoying the company of humans, other cats and dogs. However, if it becomes bored or if its lifestyle is not to its liking it may roam. Ideally, it needs a secure yard or garden or, best, a large outdoor cat pen. Not a lap cat that would be suitable for an elderly person living alone, the Bengal needs an owner who has a broad understanding of feline ways and who can provide plenty of safe space for their pet both indoors and out.

Australian Mist

A perpetual kitten, affectionate and home-loving

*Also known formerly as Spotted Mist
and Marbled Mist*

Size medium
Weight 4–7 kg (9–15½ lb)
Coat glossy, dense and soft
Lifespan 14+ years
Country of origin Australia

Colours a 'misty' (the effect is created by ticking),
creamy-mushroom background set with brown, blue,
chocolate, peach, lilac or gold spots or 'marbles'
Eyes large and almond shaped; green

This breed was developed in Victoria,
Australia, in 1977 by Dr Truda Straede by
crossing Abyssinian, Burmese and non-
pedigree shorthairs. The offspring sported
spotted coats on a ticked background. Later,
as the breeding programme progressed,
litters with marbled coats began to appear.
Now, both the spotted and the marbled
types are considered to be the same breed.
These cats are becoming increasingly popular
around the world.

The Australian Mist is a medium-sized,
solid and muscular animal with medium
bones. It has
a broad, round
head carrying fairly large ears. Its eyes are
expressive, and there is plump furring of the
medium length tail.

The really special thing about this cat is
its temperament. It is one of the best breeds
of family cat – ultra-affectionate, people-
orientated and more than happy to stay
indoors. It is gentle and amenable with
children, even young ones, other cats and
dogs, and it enjoys playing and taking part
in games. A thoroughly pleasant cat, it

would be ideal for an elderly person requiring a loyal companion or for owners living in apartments without access to gardens or yards.

Generally hardy and vigorous, the breed does not appear to be predisposed to any specific health problems. Its non-pedigree genes give it a resilient vitality.

California Spangled

Expensive and rare

Size medium
Weight 3.5–7 kg (8–15¹/₂ lb)
Coat soft; longer on belly and tail
Lifespan 12+ years
Country of origin USA

Colours Silver, Charcoal, Bronze, Gold, Red, Brown and Black
Eyes gold to brown; blue in Silvers

This is a true designer cat, bred in the 1980s to look like spotted wild cats, such as the leopard or ocelot. Paul Casey, a Hollywood screenwriter, started the breed by crossing a variety of cats, including American and British Shorthairs and Abyssinians, and his laudable, original idea was to breed a cat that resembled a leopard so that people would not want to buy and wear a fur that resembled their pet. He launched the new 'product' in the 1996 Christmas catalogue of the well-known Nieman–Marcus store at a price of $1,400 for each cat.

At present there are only a few breeders, and the breed may well be in danger of dying out. There are hardly any California Spangled cats outside the USA.

The California Spangled has a long, lean, athletic and muscular body. Rather wild-looking, it moves with a low-slung walk, and it could, indeed, be mistaken for an ocelot at first glance. Its character is by no means wild, however. It is, in fact, a very civilised and domesticated character but one that gives the impression, visually, of being bigger than it actually is. This is caused by its leopard-like spotting. The cat is rather affectionate, inquisitive and sociable and will quickly bond with its owner. Keen on eye contact, it loves to perch on places at the owner's eye level so that it can see what is going on. This cat is

intelligent and agile with a high energy level, loving to jump, run and play games with its human friends. It is equally happy at home or outside and has no specific health problems.

Who would want a California Spangled? Someone who is attracted by the idea of a rare and unusual breed and is prepared to pay a large amount of money and wait, perhaps a considerable time, for the opportunity to obtain one.

Chausie

Tough, self-reliant and sweet-natured

*Also known as Stone Cougar,
Mountain Cougar and Jungle Curl*
Size medium to large
Weight 7–8 kg (15$\frac{1}{2}$–17$\frac{1}{2}$ lb) or
more
Coat fine and smooth to coarse
Lifespan 14+ years
Country of origin USA

Colours golden, black and silver-tipped
melanistic
Eyes almond shaped and slanted; golden

This is another cat, like the Bengal, that was
developed from crossing domestic and wild
cats. In this case the wild relative is the
African jungle cat (*Felis chaus*) – hence the
name – which is one of the smaller wild cats,
weighing about 16 kg (35 lb). Found widely
across Asia, from Egypt in Africa, through
Iran, Afghanistan, Myanmar (Burma) to
Thailand, and as far as China, it prefers to live
near water and is sometimes known as the
swamp cat or reed cat.

The new breed was founded in the USA
in the 1990s by mating jungle cats with
domestic non-pedigree shorthairs. At
present, out-crosses are most commonly
with Abyssinians. Only third- or later
generation Chausies are suitable as pets.
First- and second-generation animals are
much too wild.

This is a large cat, standing up to 45 cm
(18 in) at the shoulders, with a lean, long
body and long legs, the forelegs being
slightly shorter than the hindlegs. Some
males can weigh as much as 9 kg (20 lb).
The Chausie is an Olympic athlete among
cats, being an amazingly fast runner and
able to jump 2 metres (6 feet) in a

vertical leap. Always active, it rarely sits in one place for long.

Chausies make special pets, albeit expensive ones. They have sweet natures and are affectionate, intensely loyal, alert, intelligent and fearless but not aggressive. In the family they are amenable and gentle with dogs and other cats. They need plenty of space for running and playing, either indoors or in an outdoor pen, and they are particularly fond of high places.

The breed is prone to digestive problems and cannot tolerate foods containing wheat or other gluten-containing grains. It shouldn't be given proprietary food containing cereals.

Serengeti

An affectionate family pet

Size medium to large
Weight 3.5–6.5 kg (9–14 lb)
Coat fine, soft and dense
Lifespan 12+ years
Country of origin USA

Colours Yellow to Gold Tabby, with a pattern of black or brown spots, Solid Black with or without 'ghost' spots, Silver with black spots and Black Smoke.
Eyes large and round; copper, gold, yellow or green

This is another fairly new, 'designer' breed of domestic cat that was developed to resemble a wild cat, the serval (*Leptailurus serval*), but with not a drop of serval blood in it, although its Bengal genes are to some extent inherited from wild cats. Named after the great national park in East Africa, it originated in 1994 in California when Oriental Shorthairs were crossed with Bengals.

The Serengeti is a rather tall and elegant cat that really does look like a mini-version of the serval, which is widely distributed throughout sub-Saharan Africa and is generally regarded as the most graceful of the smaller African cats. Its colours are the same as those of the Bengal (see pages 106–7).

Physically, the Serengeti has a long, lean, muscular body, which is larger and more squarely built and has bigger bones than that of the Oriental Shorthair. It has a narrow face, big ears, a long neck and long legs. It carries itself in a graceful, upright manner.

This highly intelligent cat is very talkative, emitting a wide range of squeaks, chirps, purrs and soft whistles. Gentle and outgoing, it makes a fine family cat and is sociable with children, other cats and dogs. It loves to run, climb and leap, and it must be able to go out of doors, and have space and facilities to exercise when it is indoors.

The breed is still relatively rare, but its popularity is increasing.

Sokoke

Little-known but delightful

*Also known as Sokoke Forest Cat and
Khadzonzo*
Size medium
Weight 2.5–5.5 kg (5^1/$_2$–12 lb)
Coat single-layered, shiny and dense
Lifespan 12+ years
Country of origin Kenya

Colours light brown to dark chestnut with
tabby patterns
Eyes almond shaped and slightly slanted;
amber to green in colour outlined in black

This cat originated centuries ago in the
Sokoko-Aruboko rainforest in eastern Kenya. In
the 1980s these cats were taken to Denmark
by cat lovers who admired their attractive
appearance and feared for their extinction in a
quickly shrinking natural habitat. Nowadays,
breeding programmes of Sokokes exist across
Europe and North America, although pure-
bred specimens are still relatively rare.

In many ways the Sokoke resembles an
ocelot. It has a sleek, chiselled, athletic body
with strong bone structure. The modified
wedge-shaped head, flat on top, bears a

straight nose and alert, round-tipped and,
ideally, lynx-tufted ears. Its legs are long
and elegant.

A highly intelligent and talkative cat, it
is sweet natured, affectionate and loyal as
a pet. It socializes well with the family,
although it is not generally fond of noisy
households or small children.

Anatolian Cat

Loyal and affectionate

Also known as Turkish Shorthair,
Anadolu Kedisi and Van Kedi

Size medium to large
Weight 4–6.5 kg (9–14 lb)
Coat short, smooth and
dense without any
woolly undercoat
Lifespan 12+ years
Country of origin Turkey

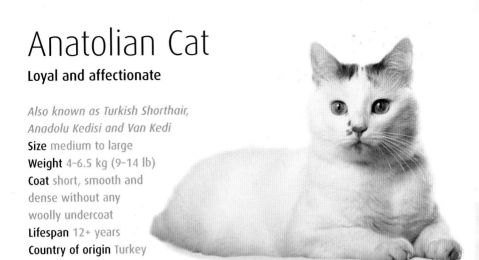

Colours all colours and all patterns
Eyes large, almond shaped and slightly slanted; green, bright yellow to dark amber or odd;
Whites can have blue eyes

This cat hails from the Anatolian region of Turkey, where it originated centuries ago. In Turkey both all-white Anatolians and Turkish Vans with blue eyes (see pages 154–5) are called Van Kedi because the Turks do not differentiate between the all-white short- and semi-longhaired varieties.

The Anatolian is a strong, well-muscled cat. The broad, modified, wedge-shaped head has large, widely set ears. The legs are in proportion to the body and end in neat, round paws, and long tail is rounded.

This is a highly active, energetic cat, and it needs plenty of space, both indoors and outside, for running and jumping. It is attracted to water, sometimes even more so than the Turkish Van. Take care to prevent the cat from scalding itself by jumping into a bath full of hot water. It is also a good idea to keep toilet lids down.

As a pet it is affectionate and loyal. It adores being petted and played with, and it hates to be left without a human or animal companion for long.

Toyger

Active and loving

Also known as California Toyger
Size medium to large
Weight 4–5.5 kg (9–12 lb)
Coat dense and soft
Lifespan 12+ years
Country of origin USA

Colours tiger-like striping of shades on brown mackerel background
Eyes small to medium sized; any colour but blue

This unusual cat really does resemble a tiger, but it weighs only about one-fiftieth of its larger relative. The breed was 'designed' by an American cat lover who crossed Bengals with non-pedigree shorthairs that showed some striped tiger features. Some of these shorthairs were homeless street cats, and one of them was actually imported from India.

The Toyger is a well-muscled, heavy-boned animal with a long body. The head is wedge shaped with a large chin and square muzzle, a long, rounded nose and small, round-tipped ears. The long tail has a black tip.

It may look fierce, but the Toyger is actually a loving, easy-going domestic animal.

As a family pet it gets on well with children and older people and, in most but not all cases, with other cats and dogs. It loves to be active, running, jumping and climbing, and so requires adequate space both indoors and out. Most Toygers enjoy going for a swim.

This is still quite a rare cat breed, and individual specimens are much more expensive than other pedigree cats. The Toyger was given its new status of Advanced New Breed by the International Cat Association (TICA) in 2006.

Kanaani

Athletic, hardy and sociable

Also known as Canaan Cat
Size medium to large
Weight 3.5–6.5 kg (9–14 lb)
Coat close lying, fine and ticked and with little undercoat
Lifespan 12+ years
Countries of origin Israel and Germany

Colours yellow-beige to cinnamon; patterns: tabby with spots and tail rings of black, chocolate or cinnamon
Eyes large and almond shaped; gooseberry-, apple- or yellow-green in colour

The word 'kanaani' means Canaanite, the name of a people mentioned in the Old Testament as living in ancient Palestine and the surrounding countries.

Breeders in Germany and elsewhere in Europe began to develop the breed in the late 1980s and early 1990s by mixing Oriental Shorthair, Abyssinian, Bengal and non-pedigree blood. The idea, apparently, was to create a cat that resembled the spotted African wild cat *Felis lybica gordonii* but had the temperament of a domestic animal.

The Kanaani is muscular and lithe. Its body is large yet slender, with a certain wild look about it that is reminiscent of the African wild cat. The head has a softly rounded forehead, and the top of the skull is flat. The ears are large, open, wide at the base and tapering, preferably with lynx-like tufted tips, and there is an M-shaped mark in the fur of the forehead. The neck is long and slender. The hindlegs are longer than the forelegs, producing a slightly raised rump.

This is an active, self-assured and playful animal that likes to be out of doors, hunting, climbing and jumping. It adapts well to indoor life if it is provided with space to run about and plenty of toys.

It has a friendly, equable temperament, and it gets on well with people, especially children, other cats and dogs, Naturally inquisitive, it likes to know what's going on in the household, though it is not as demanding of attention as, say, a Siamese.

Longhairs

Longhaired cats

Colourpoint Longhair

All domestic cats originally had short hair, so where did longhaired cats come from? Some people believe that they developed by natural selection in cold countries. The most popular theory, however, is that they arose from a spontaneous mutation, and, due to relative isolation, the new feature was perpetuated through interbreeding.

Cats with long coats were first imported into Europe from Asia Minor in the late 16th century. Today, however, most longhaired pedigree cats are descended from cats that were exported from Turkey and Persia in the late 19th century.

Most longhaired cats are of the type known as Persian. In the USA these cats are classified as Persians with the different colours listed as varieties, but in some other countries they are known as Longhairs, with each colour regarded as a separate breed.

All Persian-type Longhairs possess a sturdy, rounded body with a round face and head, large, round eyes, a short nose and short, thick legs. They all sport an exceptionally full coat composed of a soft, woolly undercoat and longer, coarser guard hairs. These can reach 12 cm (4³/4 in) long in a top show cat.

Other pedigree longhairs, including the Maine Coon and Angora, come from cold climates. Their coats are not as full as those of the Persian-type, and they are slimmer, longer in the body and leg and have narrower faces.

Cymric

White Longhair (Persian)

Fastidious and glamorous

Size medium
Weight 3-5.5 kg (6¹/₂-12 lb)
Coat lush and silky with an immense neck ruff
Lifespan 12+ years
Country of origin Persia (Iran)

Colours pure, glistening, snow white
Eyes large, round and full; copper, orange or brilliant blue

Although pure white cats of the Angora type were the first to be introduced into Europe in the 16th century, the modern White Longhair originated in the late 19th century. It was developed by crossing Angoras with Persians and was first shown in London in 1903. Since then it has steadily increased in popularity, particularly in the USA.

White Longhair cats are stocky and compact, and they have short legs with large, round paws. The heads are round and large with snub noses and neat, small, round-tipped ears set far apart and low on the head. The tails are fairly short and bushy and are carried uncurved.

White Longhairs are fastidious cats that take great pride in their appearance, constantly cleaning and grooming themselves. Even so, they must be carefully groomed by their owners everyday to prevent and remove knots. Temperamentally they are loyal and affectionate, and they make perfect pets for those confined indoors.

Black Longhair (Persian)

Affectionate and out-going

Size medium
Weight 3–5.5 kg (6½–12 lb)
Coat lush and silky with an immense neck ruff
Lifespan 12+ years
Country of origin Persia (Iran)

Colour gleaming coal-black
Eyes large, round and full; copper or orange

The Black Longhair is one of the oldest breeds, and its history stretches back to the 16th century. It is a relatively rare animal, and good specimens, unadulterated by any smokiness or rustiness of the fur, are not easy to find and are much prized.

They are similar to White Longhairs in body shape and size. The coat needs particular attention from the owner. Damp conditions can give the fur a brownish tinge, while over-exposure to sunlight may bleach it, particularly along the back.

In temperament, too, it is much like the White Longhair, but it can be suspicious of strangers. It is also said to be more lively and outgoing than its white counterpart.

Cream Longhair (Persian)

Easy-going and gentle

Size medium
Weight 3–5.5 kg
(6½–12 lb)
Coat luxuriant, thick
and silky
Lifespan 12+ years
Country of origin Persia
(Iran)

Colours buff-cream in USA; from
buttermilk to rich cream to pale
honey in Britain
Eyes large and round; copper or orange

The first Cream Longhairs probably originated from an off-white variety of the early Angoras. Later, accidental matings between Blue and Red Longhairs or, possibly, Tortoiseshells and Red Tabbies produced some pale individuals. Breeders in the USA were the first to set up programmes to develop the variety. At first, British breeders did not appreciate the new breed and nicknamed them Spoiled Oranges, a reference to the fact that Red Longhairs were originally known as Oranges.

In body shape and size they are similar to White Longhairs (see page 126). They are friendly cats with an equable temperament. They do best as indoor pets and tend to get on well with children, other cats and even dogs. These cats love to be petted, cuddled and fussed over and, like all Longhairs, need thorough grooming in two 15–30-minute daily sessions.

Probably because they tend to have small litters, Creams are less numerous than most other breeds of Longhair.

Blue Longhair (Persian)

Affectionate and even tempered

Size medium
Weight 3–5.5 kg (6½–12 lb)
Coat luxuriant, thick and silky
Lifespan 12+ years
Country of origin Persia (Iran)

Colours shades of blue
Eyes large and round; copper or orange

Although longhaired blue cats have featured in artists' impressions for centuries and were well known and appreciated in Renaissance Italy, the modern variety did not come into its own until the late 19th century. The breed, which probably originated from the cross-breeding of White and Black Longhairs, gained considerable prestige in 1901 when Queen Victoria became patron of the Blue Persian Society.

Blue Longhairs have long been one of the most popular Longhair breeds. A hundred were entered in the 1899 London Cat Show. Most Blue kittens are born with faint tabby markings, but these normally fade away after a few months.

Like the Cream Longhair, the Blue is very friendly and even tempered. They are really indoor pets and get on well with children, other cats and dogs. They like attention and must be groomed everyday.

Red Self Longhair (Persian)

Striking and colourful

Size medium
Weight 3–5.5 kg (6½–12 lb)
Coat silky and lush
Lifespan 12+ years
Country of origin
Persia (Iran); the
modern form was
developed in the
mid-20th century in
Europe and the USA

Colour deep orange-red
Eyes large and round; brilliant copper
or orange

Perfect examples of the Red Self cat are
quite rare, because most have some tabby
markings on their face, legs and tail.

Oranges, as Red Longhairs were originally
known, were being shown in Britain as early
as 1895. In the early 1930s a German
breeder produced some excellent examples
of the breed, but sadly his stock was
destroyed during the Second World War.

Red Self Longhairs have solid, cobby-type
bodies. The broad, round heads has a snub

nose and small, round-tipped ears. The legs
are short and thick set with large, round
paws. The short, fluffy tail is usually carried
straight and low.

These cats are polite and friendly, and
they make good indoor pets.

So-called Peke-faced Reds sometimes
appear as spontaneous mutations in
otherwise normal Red Self litters. Their noses
are ultra-snubs, set back in a furrowed
muzzle. This variety is controversial because
the squashed facial features may cause
breathing difficulties as well as skin
problems, and they are best avoided because
of the associated medical problems.

Blue-cream Longhair (Persian)
Engaging and extrovert

Size medium
Weight 3–5.5 kg (6^{1}/$_{2}$–12 lb)
Coat silky and lush
Lifespan 12+ years
Country of origin Persia (Iran);
the modern form was developed
in the mid-20th century in Europe
and the USA

Colour a mixture of pastel blues and creams
Eyes large and round; deep, brilliant copper
or orange

As the name implies, the Blue-cream was
developed originally by crossing Blue and
Cream pedigree Longhairs, and the coat, with
its delightful mixture of mottled cream and
pale blue-grey, has made these cats
immensely popular. There is a down side to
the colouring, however. The way in which the
colour genes are inherited means that male
Blue-creams are rare and, when they do
appear, are almost invariably sterile. The best
examples of this breed are near-perfect
examples of the cobby Longhair type.

These cats have excellent temperaments,
and they tend to be more out-going and
inquisitive than many Longhairs. However,
they are just as affectionate and amenable
as the other colours.

Chinchilla Longhair (Persian)

Desirable and glamorous

Size medium
Weight 3–5.5 kg (6½–12 lb)
Coat dense and silky
Lifespan 12+ years
Country of origin Persia (Iran); the modern form has been 'manmade' over the last 160 years

Colour snow white with black tipping
Eyes large and round; emerald green or blue-green and outlined in dark brown or black

This breed's attraction derives largely from the contrast between its white undercoat and tipped guard hairs. The rodent chinchilla has a dark undercoat tipped with white, but this cat sports the reverse coloration, which gives it a stunning, sparkling appearance.

It was one of the earliest Longhair varieties to be developed by breeders, and it had its own class in the London show in 1894.

Although it looks more delicate than other Longhairs, it is, in fact, a hardy and robust animal. The body is less cobby and with a finer bone structure than is usually seen in Longhairs. The head is round and broad with a snub nose outlined in dark brown or black and small, round-tipped ears. The legs are short, thick and very furry, and the large, round paws have black or dark brown pads. The short and bushy tail is carried straight and usually below the line of the back.

These cats possess a basically affectionate and placid disposition and their beautiful coats demand regular and meticulous grooming.

There is one variety of the Chinchilla, the Shaded Silver Longhair, whose coat carries heavier, darker tipping to form a mantle shading down the face, sides and tail.

Cameo Longhair (Persian)

A true American beauty

Size medium
Weight 3–5 kg (6¹/₂–12 lb)
Coat silky, thick and dense
Lifespan 12+ years
Country of origin USA

Colour white with cream tips; other varieties have different coloured, longer or shorter tips in combinations that produce different and dramatic coats (see below)
Eyes large and round; copper or deep orange

The modern Cameo is the product of breeding programmes established in the USA in the 1950s, and they really are among the loveliest of cats. The body is a typical cobby type. The head is round and broad with a snub nose, a pink nose pad and small, round-tipped ears. The legs are short and thick with large paws bearing pink pads. The tail is short and bushy.

The different colours and different lengths of tip produce almost magical, shimmering effects. Shell Cameos have short coloured tips that give a subtle misty effect. Shaded Cameos have longer coloured tips that glint against the white. Smoke Cameos have such long black tips that the white undercoat cannot be seen until the cat moves, creating the illusion that the cat is wreathed in vapour. The nearly matching coat and eye colours of the Cream Shaded create an irresistible combination. As in all varieties, the deepest colour should be confined to the mask, along the back and on the legs and feet.

The Cameo makes a perfect and most decorative indoor pet, with an amenable, affectionate and languorous character.

Smoke Longhair (Persian)

Tolerant and easy-going

Size medium
Weight 3–5.5 kg (6½–12 lb)
Coat silky, thick and dense
Lifespan 12+ years
Country of origin Persia (Iran)

Colours Black-tipped and Blue-tipped are the only varieties recognized in the USA and Britain; other colours of tipping, including Tortoiseshell, Lilac and Chocolate, can be found
Eyes large and round; orange or copper

One of the most delightful features of the Smoke Longhair is the way the pale undercoat shows through the dark tipping when the animal moves, creating a shimmering effect.

Smokies, as they are sometimes known, are a long-established breed, mentioned in record books from the mid-19th century and appearing in the first cat shows. They seem to have originated from chance matings between Blacks, Blues, Whites and Chinchillas. By the end of the Second World War they were almost extinct, but thankfully in the 1960s breeder interest increased in them and their future is assured.

All Tortoiseshell Smoke Longhair cats are female. Until they are a few months old solid-coloured Blacks and Smokes in the same litter are usually indistinguishable. If a Smoke is going to be a show animal, it should be kept out of bright sunlight, which will gradually bleach its coat.

These cats are relaxed and good-natured, and they make undemanding pets.

Bi-colour Longhair (Persian)

Gentle, affectionate and charming

Size medium
Weight 3–5.5 kg (6¹/₂–12 lb)
Coat dense, silky and lush
Lifespan 12+ years
Country of origin Persia (Iran)

Colours any solid colour (black, blue, red, cream, chocolate or lilac) plus white
Eyes large and round; copper or orange

The Bi-colour Longhair comes in a wonderful range of solid colours, each combined with white, the products of skilful breeding programmes. It is very much a 'designer' cat, far from a non-pedigree street cat. One of the most glamorous varieties is the Lilac-and-white Bi-colour Longhair, which is a delicate pinkish, dove grey.

The original form of the Bi-colour, the Black-and-white, was initially meant to imitate the symmetrical markings of a Dutch rabbit, but it has proved almost impossible to achieve this.

Bi-colour Longhairs have the relaxed, affectionate nature typical of most Longhairs, and they make excellent companion animals. However, as with all the other Longhairs, the coat requires regular, thorough attention to prevent it from becoming matted or forming fur balls.

In the USA, the Persian Van Bi-colour is a stunningly attractive recognized variety whose head and tail patching resembles that of the Turkish Cat. They could more correctly be called Van-patterned Persians.

Tabby Longhair (Persian)

Stunning-looking and placid

Size medium
Weight 3–5.5 kg (6¹/₂–12 lb)
Coat silky and dense
Lifespan 12+ years
Country of origin Persia (Iran)

Colours originally Brown, Red and Silver;
more recently Blue, Cream, Cameo, Patched,
Chocolate and Lilac varieties have appeared
Eyes large and round; copper or orange in all
varieties; hazel in Silver, Patched, Chocolate
and Lilac Tabbies; green also in Silver Tabbies

The Tabby Longhair first appeared in Europe
in the 17th century, although the modern
form did not emerge until the latter half of
the 19th century. It is much rarer than the
corresponding Shorthair breed.

This cat has a solid, cobby body. The round,
broad head has a short nose and small, round-
tipped ears. The legs are short and thick with
large, round feet. The tail is short and bushy.

The tabby patterning on the coat is black,
red, blue, rich cream, chocolate or lilac
depending on the variety. The pattern can be
Classic with butterfly shapes, stripes, spirals
or rings or Mackerel, which is more striped
than blotchy. A Patched or 'Torbie' pattern is
also recognized in the USA.

The Tabby Longhair has an affectionate and
gentle nature. Some owners consider it to be
more independent than most other Longhairs.

Tortoiseshell Longhair (Persian)

Gentle and beautiful

Size medium
Weight 3–5.5 kg
(6$\frac{1}{2}$–12 lb)
Coat silky and dense
Lifespan 12+ years
Country of origin Persia
(Iran)

Colour patches of red, cream and black
Eyes large and round; gleaming copper
or orange

The Tortoiseshell Longhair is a female-only breed. Shell and Shaded Tortoiseshell Longhairs are grouped together within the Shaded division in the USA; in Britain they are known as Cameos.

Longhaired cats with tortoiseshell markings were first recorded towards the end of the 19th century and appeared in cat shows in the 1900s. They probably originated from accidental matings between longhaired black cats and shorthaired tortoiseshells.

Producting the beautiful colours of the tortoiseshell is a hit-or-miss affair. Most breeders think it is best achieved by pairing two Blacks or Creams.

This cat has a similar body and build to the Tabby Longhair (see opposite).

The Tortoiseshell Longhair consistently displays an affectionate and gentle nature, and the breed has an excellent reputation for being good mothers to their kittens.

Tortoiseshell-and-white Longhair (Persian)

Eye-catching and friendly

Size medium
Weight 3–5.5 kg (6½–12 lb)
Coat dense and silky
Lifespan 12+ years
Country of origin Persia (Iran)

Colour red, cream and black or blue and cream patches against white
Eyes large and round; deep copper or orange

The Tortoiseshell-and-white is known as the Calico in the USA because its bold splashes of colour resemble the popular printed cotton.

Perhaps the most beautiful of all the Longhairs, these cats have solid, cobby bodies. The round, broad heads carry short noses and small, round-tipped ears, and the short, thick legs have large, round paws. The tail is short and bushy.

Like other tortoiseshell cats, it is a female-only breed. Its origins are obscure, but it probably arose, like the Tortoiseshell Longhair, from matings between longhaired cats and non-pedigree, shorthaired tortoiseshells.

Happy to live mainly indoors, and with a temperament that is gentle, sweet natured and friendly, it makes an ideal pet for an elderly person living alone. Although lush and dense, the fur of the Tortoiseshell-and-white Longhair is said not to become matted as easily as that of other Longhairs. This is possibly the most popular of all Longhairs.

Colourpoint Longhair (Persian)
Good-natured but spirited

Size medium
Weight 3–5.5 kg (6½–12 lb)
Coat dense and silky
Lifespan 12+ years
Countries of origin Persia (Iran); recently Sweden and the USA

Colour all point colours are possible. The most popular are Seal, Blue, Chocolate, Lilac, Red, Cream, Torties, Blue-Cream, Lilac-Cream and Tabby.
Eyes large and round; sapphire blue

Colourpoint Longhairs were first developed in Sweden and the USA in the 1920s. Later, with the carefully planned introduction of Siamese blood in the 1940s, the modern cat emerged in all its glory.

In body form and shape they are similar to the Tabby Longhair (see page 136).

These cats are gentle, sweet natured and friendly, although they can also be as spirited as the Siamese (they carry Siamese genes) but without being so demanding and loud. They are exceptionally good with children, dogs and other calm cats. They love to be cuddled and petted and are contented to live mainly indoors as highly decorative lap cats, making them make ideal pets for elderly people living alone.

Although lush and dense, the fur of the Tortoiseshell-and-white Longhair is said not to become matted as easily as that of other Longhairs, but even so they must be thoroughly groomed everyday.

Chocolate Longhair (Persian)
The ultimate 'designer' cat

Size medium
Weight 3–5.5 kg (6¹/₂–12 lb)
Coat silky, lush and thick
Lifespan 12+ years
Country of origin Persia (Iran);
recently the USA and Europe

Colours medium to dark chocolate-brown
Eyes large and round; orange or copper

At one time this cat was categorized in the USA as a solid-coloured Himalayan or Kashmir, but these descriptions have now been dropped by almost all cat associations.

Breeders encountered difficulties with the breed when they first began its development. The fur of early specimens tended to fade, the eye colour was weak, and noses and ears were too long. Colourpoint blood was subsequently introduced, and after a few years the colour stabilised and the type improved.

Chocolate Longhairs have first-class temperaments, being gentle and affectionate, and they love to be part of the family. Having inherited some of the Siamese genes carried by their Colourpoint relatives, they tend to be more outgoing and inquisitive than most Longhairs. This results in their enjoying games, such as retrieving objects thrown for them, but although they enjoy venturing outdoors from time to time, they are essentially indoor, home-loving cats. As with all the other Longhairs, thorough daily grooming is essential.

Lilac Longhair (Persian)
Decorative and companionable

Size medium
Weight 3–5.5 kg(6^1/$_2$–12 lb)
Coat silky, lush and thick
Lifespan 12+ years
Country of origin Persia (Iran);
recently the USA and Europe

Colour pinkish dove grey or lavender
Eyes large and round; orange or copper

If anything, the Lilac Longhair, which was
produced by introducing blue genes into
breeding lines, proved even more elusive
than the Chocolate (see opposite), and it is
still relatively rare.

These cats have excellent temperaments.
They are affectionate and gentle and enjoy
being part of the family. Like the Chocolate
and having inherited some of the Siamese
genes carried by their Colourpoint relatives,
they tend to be more outgoing and
inquisitive than is usual for Longhairs,
enjoying the same type of games as the
Chocolate.

The beautiful coat requires thorough, daily
grooming to keep it in tip-top condition.

Cymric

Independent, affectionate and brave

Also known as Longhaired Manx
Size medium
Weight 3.5–5.5 kg (8–12 lb)
Coat medium-long, soft and heavy
double coat
Lifespan 12+ years
Country of origin Isle of Man (off the
north-west coat of England)

Colours all colours and patterns. Some cat associations do not recognize Colourpoints
(Himalayan pattern), Lavender, Chocolate, Lavender with white and Chocolate with white.
Eyes large and round; any colour to complement the coat

The origin of the name Cymric lies in the Welsh word *Cymru*, which means Wales, although the cat has no known connection with that country.

Cymrics are essentially longhaired Manx cats (see pages 66–7). At one time longhaired kittens born to Manx cats were considered to be unwelcome mutants and discarded, and it was only in the 1960s, when similar mutations occurred in American and Canadian litters, that they began to receive the attention they deserved and breeding programmes were set up. The new breed started to become popular in the mid-1970s, but it is still fairly rare.

The body of the Cymric is the same as that of the Manx and, as with that breed, there are truly tailless Rumpies, Risers, Stumpies or Stubbies as well as Longies, all named according to their tail length.

These cats can take up to five years to mature fully. They are active, intelligent, fun-loving animals, and they get on well with children and also with other cats and dogs if brought up with them. A Cymric will be proud and protective towards its home and will not be afraid to send any interloping pet packing.

It is loyal and affectionate and relishes being a family member, and although it prefers a quiet household, it will adapt to a bustling environment. A keen hunter, it makes a first-class mouser. A Cymric's coat should be groomed thoroughly at least once a week so that it does not become knotted and matted.

Semi-longhairs and hairless types

Semi-longhaired & hairless cats

Semi-longhaired breeds of cat might better be described as medium-length-haired. Most of them originated in cross-breeding programmes of Longhair and Shorthair types. This is a highly varied group, and it contains what many people consider to be some of the most attractive and interesting cats.

Among them are rugged, country-loving types, such as the Norwegian Forest Cat (see pages 164–5), glamorous exotics, such as the Balinese (see pages 152–3), highly popular family pets in the shape of the Ragdoll (see pages 150–51), and fascinating curiosities, such as the Munchkin (see pages 178–9).

Norwegian Forest Cat

The coats of all Semi-longhair cats need regular, careful grooming to keep them free from mats and tangles.

Hairless breeds include the Sphynx (see pages 184–5) and Peterbald (see page 187). At one time it was thought by many cat owners that these cats, and also the Devon and Cornish Rex (see pages 94–5 and 96–7), were the best pets for people believed to be allergic to cats. A common belief was that allergic incidents, such as asthma attacks and hay fever-like symptoms, were the result of the patient breathing in small particles of cat fur. Therefore, it was suggested, if you must have a cat you should get a Rex or a Sphynx. Sadly, because of this advice, many innocent, furry feline companions were disposed of. Now we know that the real problem lies in the cat's – all cats' – saliva, which contains a protein that acts as an allergy provoker in a relatively small number of susceptible humans. When the saliva is deposited on the animal's skin as it washes itself, it dries to form a kind of dandruff, and it is this that sometimes triggers an allergic response when the cat is stroked or brushed. Hairless cats produce less of the dandruff than hairy ones when they wash themselves, but they can, nevertheless, produce enough to stimulate some degree of

Somali

allergic response. Happily, most people do not have the slightest problem when grooming, stroking or cuddling their family pet.

Before you buy a hairless cat, remember that their need for extra calories to keep warm tends to make them eat more than furry cats of the same weight. And, in winter, try to persuade a family member to knit a woolly jumper of some sort for the pet.

Birman

Beautiful and gentle

Size medium
Weight 2.5–6 kg (5½–13 lb)
Coat semi-longhair; silky and fluffy
Lifespan 14+ years
Country of origin Burma (Myanmar)

Colours beige-gold or bluish-white with points reminiscent of the Siamese, of various colours, including seal-brown (Seal-point), chocolate (Chocolate-point), blue-grey (Blue-point) and pink-tinged grey (Lilac-point); the front paws are tipped with white, and the back paws have white gloves at the front and white gauntlets at the rear, finishing in a point up the back of the legs
Eyes almost round, set well apart and slightly slanted; sapphire blue

The Siamese may well have been involved in the development of the Birman, but Burmese tradition has its own story to tell of its origins. Before the birth of the Lord Buddha a sacred Burmese temple containing pure white cats came under attack, during which the high priest collapsed and died. His favourite cat at once jumped on to the old man's head and was suddenly transformed: its coat became golden with points the colour of the Burmese soil, and its eyes turned blue. Where the cat's paws touched the priest the fur remained white, a symbol of goodness. (Birmans do indeed display white 'socks' on all four feet.) Encouraged by the miracle, the remaining priests were able to fend off the invaders.

The cat's recent history is almost as colourful. In 1919 two of these cats were sent to a Major Gordon Russell in France as a token of gratitude from the priests he had helped escape from Tibet, and these animals founded the breed in the West.

The body is strongly built, elongated but still quite stocky, neither svelte nor cobby. The head is fairly round and broad with full cheeks and a medium-length nose. The medium-sized, round-tipped ears are almost as wide at the base as they are tall. The legs are medium length and thick set with large, round paws, and the tail is medium length, bushy, but longer and finer than in most Longhairs.

Birmans are highly amenable, civilized and gentle, enjoying family life and adapting well to other pets, including dogs.

Some cat books suggest that the Birman's fur doesn't matt. This is not true; it does. These cats need regular – at least twice weekly – brushing and combing.

Ragdoll

Big and floppy

Size large
Weight 4.5–9 kg (10–20 lb)
Coat long, full and silky
Lifespan 14+ years
Country of origin USA

Colour pale fawn with colour points; recognized coat patterns include the Bi-colour (pale body, white chest, underbelly and legs, and dark, mask, ears and tail), the Colourpoint (pale body and darker points) and the Mitted (a Colourpoint with white chest, bib, chin and front paw 'mittens')
Eyes blue

The Ragdoll is one of the larger breeds of cat, somewhat similar in appearance to the Birman. When it is picked up, however, it is not at all Birman-like: it relaxes all its muscles to become weak as a kitten and as floppy as the doll from which it takes its name. It will lie draped over your arm like a waiter's napkin.

The breed originated in California in the 1960s from the crossing of White Persian (Angora) cats and Birmans, with Burmese blood being subsequently introduced. It used to be widely believed that Ragdolls had a high tolerance to pain because the original founders of the breed were born to a long-haired queen that had been injured in a car accident. In fact, this is complete nonsense. Researchers still cannot explain the 'floppiness' that the cat exhibits, and physiological tests have detected no difference between the Ragdoll and other breeds.

The cat has a powerful and imposing physique with a long, muscular body, sturdy legs and large, round paws.

The Ragdoll is sweet natured and extremely tolerant of the whims and foibles of others, quickly becoming devoted to its owner. It likes company, both human and canine, and is good with children and other cats. Although fond of going outside, Ragdolls make first-class indoor pets, thriving on and bestowing abundant affection in equal measure. They can do well in urban apartments.

Another myth about the breed is that the coat tends not to matt. It can and it does, and these cats need regular grooming.

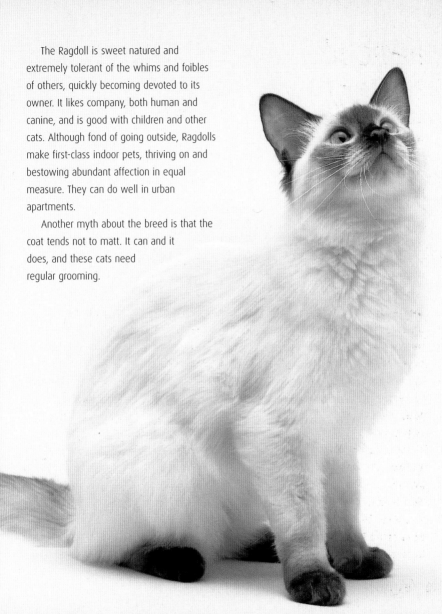

Balinese

Playful, elegant and companionable

Size medium
Weight 3–4 kg (6½–9 lb)
Coat fine and silky with a tendency to
wave where it is longest; no soft
undercoat
Lifespan 14+ years
Country of origin USA

Colours all the Siamese colours (see pages 68–9); some US cat associations use the name
Javanese for varieties in non-Siamese recognized colours
Eyes medium sized and almond shaped; sapphire blue

The breed has no connection with the Indonesian holiday island of Bali. It was given its name because of the way its graceful tail plume sways from side to side when as it walks with its tail held erect. The effect is reminiscent of a Balinese dancer's movement.

The cat inherits its natural elegance from its Siamese origins, from which it also gets the long, svelte body, wedge-shaped head and enchanting blue eyes. It can, in fact, be considered a long-haired Siamese, and the foundation of the Balinese breed was almost certainly Siamese parents carrying a random genetic mutation for long hair.

The breed first appeared in the USA in the late 1940s and was accepted for championship by all US associations by 1970. The Balinese has a body that is lithe but still strong and muscular. The head is a long, tapering, wedge shape with a long, straight nose and large, pointed ears that are wide at the base. The legs are long and slim, the forelegs being somewhat shorter than the hindlegs. The paws are neat, small and oval. The tail is long and thin with a fine point, and its fur should spread out like a lush plume.

Balinese cats are less noisy and boisterous than Siamese, but they are affectionate and playful, particularly with their offspring. They have excellent temperaments, chat a lot and adapt well to any household environment. They get on well with children, other cats and dogs and hate being left alone for long, so if family members are out at work during the day it is generally best to consider having a pair of these cats so that they can keep each other entertained.

Turkish Van

Water-loving and intelligent

Also known as Van Kedi, Turkish Cat, White Turk and Turkish Swimming Cat
Size large
Weight 4–8 kg (9–18 lb)
Coat long and silky
Lifespan 14+ years
Country of origin Turkey

Colour chalk white with colour markings on the head, base of the ears and tail; the usual colour marking is auburn, but most other colours are acceptable
Eyes amber, blue or odd

The cat takes its name from the area around Lake Van in southeastern Turkey, where it has been domesticated for several hundred years and happily goes swimming in shallow streams and pools. Its popularity has grown in recent years, especially in Australia and the USA. No other cat has markings quite like those of this breed, and the white, thumb-like blaze on its forehead is said by the Turkish people to symbolize the mark of Allah.

Vans have long, muscular bodies, a short, wedge-shaped head with a long nose and pink nose pad, large, pointed and tufted ears and pink-rimmed eyes. The muscular legs are of medium length with small, neat, round feet bearing pink pads. The tail is long and feathery.

Coming from a region of Turkey that is extremely cold in winter but hot in summer, these cats moult profusely during warm spells and can look virtually shorthair in appearance.

Because of the cat's fascination with water, owners should be careful to run baths cold before they add hot water

in case their pet slips into the bathroom, jumps into the water and scalds itself badly. Also, it is advisable to keep toilet lids down. If you have a pool or pond in the garden try to arrange some form of stepped or sloping edge to enable the cat to climb out, should it venture in. If the cat has unsupervised access to the garden, consider having a net cover.

Affectionate, lively, highly intelligent and with a soft voice, the Van makes an excellent companion. It is easy-going and sociable with dogs and other cats, but it intensely dislikes being over-enthusiastically or roughly handled. Blue-eyed Vans may be deaf.

Angora

Playful and attractive

Also known as Turkish Angora
Size small to medium
Weight 2–4 kg (4¹⁄₂–9 lb)
Coat medium-long, very fine and silky with a tendency to wave; there should be a well-developed and lush ruff
Lifespan 14+ years
Country of origin Turkey, particularly the area around Ankara (formerly Angora), but may have arrived in that country with Vikings

Colours most of the Longhair coat colours, including white, black, blue, tabby, calico and bi-colour
Eyes medium to large, almond shaped and slanted; blue, green, hazel, amber, copper or odd

The Angora may well have been the first Longhair to be seen in Europe. Turkish sultans were sending these cats as gifts to the nobles of France and England during the 16th century, but by the end of the 19th century they had fallen out of fashion, being ousted by the new Longhairs. Happily the zoo in Turkey's capital city, Ankara, came to the rescue, and the Angora became something of a protected species. In the early 1960s an American couple purchased two of the cats from the zoo and re-established the breed in the USA, where it is now popular.

Angoras in Britain were developed artificially from breeding programmes using Siamese blood rather than by importing Turkish stock. These cats look the same as the original and American Angoras, but they have a more querulous tone of voice.

The Angora's body is lithe and athletic. It has a small to medium-sized, wedge-shaped head with a long nose and large ears, which are wide at the base and pointed. The legs are long and slim, the forelegs being shorter than the hindlegs, and these end in small, round, dainty paws. The long, tapering tail is frequently carried proudly curled over the back, almost touching the ears.

This is a most gentle, affectionate and intelligent cat. It loves to have play games, climb, run and leap, and its ideal owner will be able to provide peace and quiet as well as plenty of space and opportunities for the cat to exercise itself. Angoras aren't keen on noisy households or ones with young children constantly dashing about.

Tiffany

Gentle, inquisitive and outgoing

Also known as Chantilly and Tiffany-Chantilly
Size medium
Weight 2.5–4.5 kg (5½–10 lb)
Coat long and silky
Lifespan 12+ years
Country of origin USA

Colours warm sable brown (most popular); also black, cinnamon, blue, lilac and fawn; various coat patterns
Eyes round, slightly slanted and set wide apart with an expressive look; golden in colour

Essentially a long-haired Burmese and still relatively rare, the Tiffany has the elegant combination of an Oriental body type with a luxuriously long, silky coat. It was developed in New York and later in Canada between 1967 and 1987 by crossing Burmese cats with Longhairs.

The Tiffany has a medium-sized body, which is more muscular and rounded than that of a Siamese. The head is rounded with a shortish nose, firmly rounded chin and medium-sized ears, which are set well apart and are slightly rounded at the tips, carrying long 'streamers'. The legs are long and slim with oval to round paws, and the tail is of medium length and bushy.

Tiffany kittens are born a *café au lait* colour, which darkens gradually into the mature coat, although this is still lighter in tone than that of a Burmese.

This is a loving, loyal cat, which will be devoted to its owner. Not too demanding or mischievous, it is not as placid as a Persian

nor as active as an Oriental. It is sociable and will quickly make friends with children, other cats and dogs, but it can initially be rather reticent with strangers. It is quite talkative, with a vocabulary of soft trills and chirps.

The breed is a healthy one, with no specific problems and requiring minimal care, and the silky, little-shedding and non-matting coat needs only occasional combing. However, the ears tend to become waxy and must be cleaned regularly.

The Tiffany is not to be confused with the Tiffanie, a breed created by crossing Burmese and Chinchillas.

Somali

Wild-looking but good-tempered

*Also known as Longhaired Abyssinian
and Fox Cat*
Size medium
Weight 3–5.5 kg (6$^{1}/_{2}$–12 lb)
Coat medium-long, dense, silky and
fine-textured; the undercoat is pale
ticked with chocolate to give a silver-
peach effect
Lifespan 14+ years
Country of origin USA

Colours 28 colour variations, identical to those of the Abyssinian (see pages 72–3); the most
commonly seen are the Usual or Ruddy (golden-brown coat ticked with black) and the Sorrel
or Red (warm copper ticked with chocolate)
Eyes large and almond shaped; amber, hazel or green outlined in black

This is an impressive, rather wild-looking cat that has, one might easily imagine, just walked out of an ancient forest.

Essentially a long-haired Abyssinian, the Somali has a lush, slightly shaggy coat without any tendency to woolliness. Whereas Abyssinian coat hairs have two or three bands of colour that form the ticking, the longer Somali hairs carry 10 or more bands, which create an intensely rich colour density.

Longhaired genes may have been introduced into Abyssinian lines in the 1930s or even before, but it was not until the 1960s that the breed was systematically developed in the USA. Somalis are now widely distributed across Europe and are particularly popular in Australia.

The Somali has an Oriental-type, medium-length, elegant body that is slightly larger than that of an Abyssinian and not as fine-boned as a Siamese. The head is a moderate wedge shape with a medium-sized nose and large, pointed ears set well apart and tufted. The legs are long and slender, and the paws are small and oval with pink pads and tufts between the toes. The tail is long, thick at the base and slightly tapering, and carries a full brush.

These are bright, active, good-tempered and independent cats. They are slightly shyer than Abyssinians, but are utterly unsuited to a life spent entirely indoors. They must be able to indulge their remarkable athletic abilities by running, climbing and jumping, and this means providing lots of space in the house or, perhaps, a large, secure outdoor pen with snug housing. When resting between bouts of activity they love to be warm.

Although shy and reticent at first, they quickly develop strong bonds with their owner and become affectionate with people they trust.

Maine Coon

Big cat, big personality

Size large
Weight 3.5–8 kg (8–18 lb)
Coat thick and shaggy yet silky
Lifespan 12+ years
Country of origin USA

Colours all except Chocolate and Lilac points and Colourpoints, but most often copper-brown marked in black
Eyes large, slightly slanted and set well apart; green, gold or copper in colour; Whites can have blue or odd eyes

The Maine Coon is the oldest American breed. It may well have roamed free in the state of Maine in the early days of its history, drawing comparisons to the indigenous raccoon, which has a similar appearance to tabby-type Maine Coons and similar hunting habits. (The raccoon is, of course, a totally different species to which the Maine Coon cannot possibly be related.)

It is probable that the forebears of the breed were robust American farm cats and longhaired cats brought back to Maine by sailors and traders from Europe. The breed was shown at the 1860 New York Cat Show and won the Madison Square Garden Show of 1895. From then on its popularity decreased as Persians were introduced into the USA, but its fortunes revived again in the 1950s.

The harsh New England climate contributed to the development of the cat's thick coat, a feature it shares with that other cold-climate cat, the Norwegian Forest Cat (see pages 164–5). The Maine Coon's body is large, long and well-muscled, and in silhouette the shape is almost rectangular. The wedge-shaped head, though fairly large, is small in proportion to the body and has a medium-long nose and large ears, which taper to a point. The legs are of medium length and strong with large, round paws. The tail is about as long as the body, with a wide base and a blunt, plume-like end.

This is a most friendly, companionable cat with two characteristic behaviours. It loves to sleep rough and is often found curled up in the oddest positions and in the oddest places. In addition, it 'talks' with the most charming, quiet, chirping sound.

Maine Coons need plenty of space, either in the country, where they can roam freely, or in town, where they are happy to live indoors but should be provided with an outdoor pen.

Norwegian Forest Cat

Hardy and independent

*Also known as Norsk Skaukatt, Norsk
Skogkatt and Wegie*

Size large
Weight 6–9 kg (13–20 lb)
Coat long, smooth and shaggy with a
woolly undercoat
Lifespan 12+ years
Country of origin Norway

Colours all colours and patterns, although British and some other countries' cat fancies don't
allow Chocolate, Lilac or Colourpoint for showing
Eyes any colour

In Norse legend the Norwegian Forest
Cat is a mysterious, enchanted animal,
probably none other than the troll cat of
Scandinavian fairy tales. It is certainly a
natural old breed, a hardy, rugged character
that is well adapted to bitter Scandinavian
winters. The thick double, water-resistant
coat, blue with white showing through,
keeps out wind and snow, keeps in warmth
and, after being drenched, dries out in
about 15 minutes. Regular and thorough
grooming is essential to keep the coat in
good condition.

These cats love people, but they demand
a lot of attention. In return, they provide
intelligent, friendly, playful company. A curious
characteristic of the breed is that it tends to
come down from trees spirally, head first.

Although basically a cat of the outdoors,
where it can indulge its skills as a fine, swift
hunter and its fascination for running water –
it will try its paw at fishing in shallow pools
and streams – it will adapt happily to living
indoors as long as it has plenty of space.
Nevertheless, this is not a cat that should be
kept in a high-rise apartment.

Japanese Bobtail
Sociable and good-natured

Size small to medium
Weight 2.5–4 kg (5 1/2–9 lb)
Coat soft, silky and medium length
Lifespan 12+ years
Country of origin Japan

Colours any except Silver, Ticked Tabby and Colourpoint; Red and White and Black and White are most common, and the most popular is the three-coloured red, black and white, known as Mi-Ke (Japanese for 'three colour')
Eyes large and oval; of any colour, but odd eyes are particularly prized

The Japanese Bobtail was named both for its country of origin and its powder-puff, rabbit-type tail. Its roots can be traced back in the Far East to the 7th century, and it was not until the late 1960s that Americans set the pedigree standard.

The medium-sized body is lean and elegant. The triangular head has a long nose with a pad matching the coat colour. The round-tipped ears are large and set well apart and at right angles to the head. The legs are long and slender with the hindlegs longer than the forelegs. Paws are medium in size and oval with pads matching the coat colour. The tail is short and curled.

When they are sitting Bobtails often raise one paw, a gesture that is believed to bring good luck. Called *maneki-neko* (beckoning cats). Prints and models of them are often displayed by Japanese people and shop doorways to welcome visitors. The façade of the Gotokuji temple in Tokyo is decorated with these cats, all with one paw lifted, to greet worshippers.

This cat is hardy and generally healthy, happy to be inside or out and keen on climbing and playing. It is sweet natured and sociable with humans, dogs and other cats. It is quite talkative and adores being cuddled and playing with its owner.

Nebelung

Rare, intelligent and companionable

Also known as Nibelung
Size medium
Weight 2.5–4 kg (5¹/₂–9 lb)
Coat lustrous, silky, fine and double-layered
Lifespan 14+ years
Country of origin USA

Colour misty blue tipped with silver
Eyes green

The Nebelung is named after the 'creature of the mist' of Nordic legend and Wagner's opera *Der Ring des Nibelungen* (The Ring of the Nebelungs).

The cat, which resembles a longhaired Russian Blue, was developed in the mid-1980s from a mating between a black, non-pedigree shorthair and a Russian Blue, which produced a blue semi-longhaired kitten. The next litter came up with a blue semi-longhaired female kitten. Once matured, the two siblings were mated, and the breeding programme continued, with more Russian Blue blood of various coat types being introduced. The breed is nowadays steadily increasing in popularity in the USA, Russia, the Netherlands and Germany.

Nebelungs are sturdy animals with long, muscular, rather elegant bodies. They have long legs and oval paws with generous tufting between the toes, and the long, plumed tails are as long as the body length from rump to shoulder blades. The head is basically wedge shaped, bearing large ears and a long, straight nose, but it has been described as cobra-like because of the way the ears are set far to the back of the skull and curve slightly forwards to form a hood.

Generally quiet, gentle and affectionate, the Nebelung can be rather suspicious of

strangers. It is best as an indoor pet as long as it has plenty of space. It loves to play and climb, though it is not keen on noisy, bustling households and generally dislikes over-enthusiastic handling. Many owners claim that Nebelungs rarely sharpen their claws on things – which is a desirable trait, if true.

A Nebelung should be groomed at least twice a week.

Scottish Fold

Gentle and sociable

Also known as Coupari
Size medium to large
Weight 2.5–6 kg (5¹/₂–13 lb)
Coat thick, soft and dense
Lifespan 12+ years
Country of origin Scotland

Colours any; Lilac, Colourpoint and Chocolate are not accepted by some organisations for showing
Eyes any colour in keeping with the coat

The unique and immediately obvious feature of the Scottish Fold is its forward-folded ears. If records are correct, the gene for folded ears has been present in the domestic cat population for about 170 years, but the modern Scottish Fold arose from a mutant white kitten named Susie, who was found at a farm in 1966 in Perthshire in Scotland, from where it was exported to the USA in the early 1970s.

The folded-ear gene is also involved in some way with bone development, and skeletal abnormalities are likely to develop if two cats carrying the gene are mated. To avoid such problems, Scottish Folds are mated only to straight-eared cats and never to another Fold. Kittens with normal ears produced by Scottish Folds are called Scottish Straights. Other interesting combinations are the Foldex, a Canadian crossing of a Scottish Fold and an Exotic Shorthair, and the extremely rare Scottish Fold Longhair, a crossing of a Scottish Fold with a British Shorthair carrying the Persian gene.

Scottish Folds are delightful, gentle, affectionate and playful animals. Their bodies are compact and powerfully built, and they have short, stocky legs. The ears may be tightly or loosely folded, but the ear opening should be completely covered. The characteristic does not make these cats hard of hearing.

They are quiet, self-assured animals, which socialize well with other cats, dogs and children. Scottish Folds like to be part of the family and enjoy interactive play with their owners, but they are unenthusiastic about being left alone. If all family members go out to work it is best to have two cats so that they can keep each other company.

American Bobtail
Talkative and playful

Size medium to large
Weight 3–8 kg (6¹/2–16 lb)
Coat double coat with a soft, thick topcoat and a downy undercoat, which comes in two forms: a medium-length longhair and a water-resistant, medium-length longhair
Lifespan 14+ years
Country of origin USA

Colours all colours and patterns
Eyes large and almond shaped; any colour

The breed was created in Arizona in the mid-1960s when a bobtailed non-pedigree cat was crossed with a Siamese. Blood from other non-pedigree and Colourpoint (Himalayan) Persians was subsequently introduced with the short tail and attractive markings reappearing.

The Bobtail possesses a well-muscled, cobby, athletic body. The broad, wedge-shaped head carries ears that have plenty of hair inside and tufted tips and a distinct brow above the eyes. The natural 'powder-puff' tail can be slightly curved and stands up when the animal is alert. The cat walks with a rolling gait, similar to that of a bobtailed wildcat.

Although this cat has a definite look of the wild, it is, in fact, one of the most loving, gentle and intelligent of breeds. It loves family life and gets on well with other animals and, especially, with children. Natural clowns, they are constantly initiating games with their owners, and they tend, delightfully, to purr a lot. Their pleasure in playing is demonstrated by the trilling, chirping, clicking noises they make when they are happy. Curiously, they seem to have a magpie-like fascination for shiny objects, which they may try to purloin, so you should also keep your jewellery boxes firmly closed.

The American Bobtail enjoys going out for walks and is easily trained to the lead. It quickly adapts to riding in vehicles – indeed, some long-haul truck drivers like to have them in the cab as travelling companions.

Bobtails take up to three years to mature fully.

American Curl

Gentle and affectionate

Size medium
Weight 2.5–4.5 kg (5½–10 lb)
Coat soft, silky and lying flat with little or no undercoat; there are longhaired and shorthaired varieties
Lifespan 14+ years
Country of origin USA

Colours all colours and patterns
Eyes all colours

This cat may be distinguished by its unique ears, which curl backwards, giving the animal an alert, perky, ready-to-play expression.

The original American Curl was Shulasmith, a stray longhaired black female cat that dropped in on the Ruga family in Lakewood, California, in 1981 and decided to stay. Although still an uncommon breed, it can now be found in many countries across the world.

American Curl kittens are born with straight ears, which begin to curl after about 10 days.

These cats are highly intelligent and inquisitive, and they make faithful and people-oriented pets, which bond remarkably quickly with children, other cats and dogs. They will follow their owner around, not wanting to miss anything that may be going on. Although not particularly talkative, they do make trill-like, cooing sounds when they come across something that interests them. One of their most attractive features is the fact that they retain their kittenish personality throughout adulthood. They love being seen 'helping' around the house.

LaPerm

Inquisitive and demanding

Size small to medium
Weight 2–4.5 kg (5½–10 lb)
Coat soft and wavy, curly or straight with no undercoat
Lifespan 14+ years
Country of origin USA

Colours all colours
Eyes all colours, including odd-eyed

The year after the American Curl first came on the scene, it was the state of Oregon that produced the next new breed. The founder of the LaPerm breed was a natural, spontaneous mutation in a litter born to a grey tabby cat, Speedy, which lived on a farm.

Kittens can be born with any one of three coat types: straight, curly or bald. Straight-haired kittens tend to stay straight coated throughout their lives. If the coat and whiskers are curly or the kitten is bald with curly whiskers, it will become a curly-coated adult.

These cats are affectionate and love to be cuddled. They have the habit of rubbing their faces or paws against your head, neck and face, and will return kisses.

But LaPerms are not just big softies. They are highly inquisitive cats, which enjoy hunting and quickly learn to retrieve objects that are thrown for them. Gentle and quiet-voiced, they can be much more vocal when they want attention. Because of their strong loyalty and attachment to their owners they make excellent indoor pets for apartment dwellers. Their playful, kittenish temperament is a continual source of entertainment to their owners.

Pixie-Bob

'The best pet cat in the world'

Size medium to large
Weight 3.5–9 kg (8–20 lb)
Coat semi-dense, soft and weatherproof
Lifespan 12+ years
Country of origin USA

Colours Brown Spotted Tabby is the only accepted form for showing, but other variations are Russet, Fawn and Tan
Eyes triangular in shape; blue as kittens, changing to green-gold, then gold or golden brown when several months old

This breed was initially believed to be the progeny of wild American bobcats that had mated with domestic cats. However, DNA testing proved that these cats do not carry bobcat genes but are of wholly domestic origin.

In 1985 Carol Ann Brewer, who lived in Washington state, obtained a spotted male kitten with a short tail like a bobcat. The next year she rescued another rather large cat, also with a bobcat tail. This tom mated with a wild-looking, brown-spotted female belonging to one of her neighbours, and a litter arrived from this mating. Ms Brewer kept one of the kittens, named Pixie, and a year or so later she began a breeding programme with Pixie as the foundation cat. Subsequently, almost two dozen cats from the same area, which were believed to be bobcat and domestic cat crosses, were introduced into the line, and other US cat breeders joined in the scheme by working with a range of wild-looking barn cats. Thus was established the Pixie-Bob.

The first representatives of the breed arrived in Europe in 2001.

Pixie-Bobs are big cats with pear-shaped heads. They have black fur and skin on the

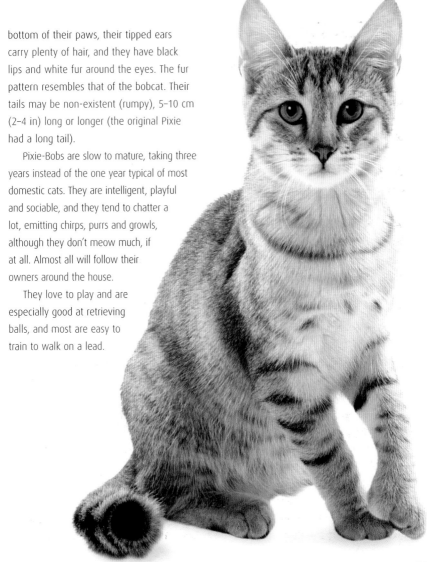

bottom of their paws, their tipped ears carry plenty of hair, and they have black lips and white fur around the eyes. The fur pattern resembles that of the bobcat. Their tails may be non-existent (rumpy), 5–10 cm (2–4 in) long or longer (the original Pixie had a long tail).

Pixie-Bobs are slow to mature, taking three years instead of the one year typical of most domestic cats. They are intelligent, playful and sociable, and they tend to chatter a lot, emitting chirps, purrs and growls, although they don't meow much, if at all. Almost all will follow their owners around the house.

They love to play and are especially good at retrieving balls, and most are easy to train to walk on a lead.

Munchkin

Appealing and inquisitive

Size small
Weight 1.5–3.5 kg (3¹/₂–8 lb)
Coat variable, depending on breeding; Shorthair varieties are commoner than Semi-longhairs
Lifespan 10+ years
Country of origin USA

Colours any colour
Eyes large and oval; any colour

Munchkins are cats with very short legs, and they are descended from either pedigree or non-pedigree forebears. Named after the little folk in *The Wizard of Oz*, they are a fairly new breed, created by a genetic mutation that affects the leg bones. Since the breed first appeared in the 1980s, when an extremely short-legged black cat was found living under a mobile home in Louisiana, many more spontaneous Munchkin-type mutations have appeared, some of them in pedigree cats.

Only a few cat registries recognize the breed. Others do not, considering them to be genetically diseased and suffering from the skeletal abnormality known as achondroplasia, a condition deforming the long bones of the leg.

Munchkin breeders and enthusiasts, however, claim that they are a sound breed, which is not especially susceptible to health problems and is ideal for small households. Depending on their genetic make-up, the offspring of a Munchkin mated with a non-Munchkin may contain all Munchkin kittens, all normal kittens or a combination of the two. A litter produced by two Munchkin parents may be all Munchkins, all normal kittens, all non-viable kittens or any combination of the foregoing.

Munchkins are agile, quick-moving cats, with cheerful, sweet-natured dispositions, and they socialize well with children, other cats and dogs. Because of their size, however, they intensely dislike being harassed by bigger creatures. They are generally hardy animals with a great interest in the world around them, and their inquisitive nature frequently leads them to purloin and hide items of interest. To get a better view of their surroundings they sometimes perch up on their haunches.

This little cat is ideal for people living in urban apartments who require an affectionate and loyal indoor pet. When they are outside, however, the cat should be penned for its own safety.

There are a number of Munchkin variations nowadays to be found. Munchkins crossed with Persians and Munchkins crossed with Exotic Shorthairs are called Napoleans.

Skookum

Small and loving

Size small
Weight 2.5–3.5 kg (5¹/₂–8 lb)
Coat semi-long, short and curly
Lifespan 10+ years
Country of origin USA

Colours any, including Colourpoint
Eyes large and almond shaped; any colour

The Native American Chinook word Skookum means great, powerful or mighty, which is not bad for such a little fellow. Like the ten other breeds of dwarf cat, the Skookum was created in the late 1980s by crossing Munchkins with cats possessing normal legs, in this case the LaPerm (see page 175). Like the LaPerm, one of the Rex cat breeds, the Skookum has a curly coat that does not shed much. Its hindlegs are distinctly longer than its forelegs.

This cat is intelligent, sociable, playful and affectionate. Agile and quick-moving, like its relative the Munchkin, the Skookum is, believe it or not, a rather efficient hunter, which loves to jump about. It mixes well with children, dogs and other cats and

makes yet another perfect indoor cat, but one that can be allowed out of doors if confined to a large pen.

Mating two Skookums together is a lucky dip as far as what the resulting kittens may look like. Because of their varied genetic make-up a mixed litter of LaPerms, Munchkins, Skookums and some that have neither a curly coat nor short legs may be produced.

Highland Lynx

Energetic and intelligent

Size large
Weight 6–9 kg (13–20 lb)
Coat soft to medium-hard with a thick undercoat; both long and short hair
Lifespan 12+ years
Country of origin USA

Colours Sorrel, Ebony, Chocolate, Fawn, Silver, Snow, Bronze, Blue, Lilac and Sepia Brown; Marbled Tabby (Clouded Leopard), Ticked Agouti (Tawny) and Spotted Tabby (Leopard Spotted) patterns
Eyes gold to green; blue in Snows

The Highland Lynx originated in the USA in 1995 from a cross between the Desert Lynx and the Chausie (see pages 112–13) and domestic breeds, including curled-eared domestics.

This is a stocky, strong, hard-bodied cat with curled-back ears, thick legs and large, tufted paws. Its tail length varies from none at all to halfway to the ground. Some individuals exhibit polydactyly – that is, they have six toes instead of four on each foot. Although completely domesticated, it physically resembles the North American bobcat, a cat that is considerably smaller than the Canadian lynx and one, incidentally, that is unceasingly hunted by that larger feline, the puma.

The Highland Lynx is an energetic, intelligent cat and not very vocal. It is, in fact, a rather dog-like animal, which loves running, climbing and playing. It is affectionate and bonds closely with people it knows, and it gets on well with children, other cats and dogs. Obviously, it must be provided with plenty of secure space, both indoors and out, in order to cater for its active lifestyle.

Sphynx
Hairless and affectionate

Also known as Canadian Sphynx,
Canadian Hairless, Moon Cat and
Temple Cat
Size medium
Weight 3–4 kg (6^1/$_2$–9 lb)
Coat none
Lifespan 12+ years
Country of origin Canada

Colours any recognized colour or pattern
Eyes deep set, lemon shaped and slanted; the colour should complement the skin

Although hairless cats are said to have been bred by the Aztecs, the modern Sphynx, which has been unkindly called 'a suede hot-water bottle', is of fairly recent origin, the first specimen being a mutant kitten, Prune, which was born in Ontario, Canada, in 1966. Sadly, Prune had no offspring, but in 1967 another litter of hairless kittens was born to a rescued longhaired queen, again in Canada.

The breed, which is still rare outside North America, has a variety of coat colours and patterns. The ears are very large, and there are no whiskers. Although described as hairless, the skin may actually have a thin layer of very soft hair, rather like the fuzz on peach skin.

The Sphynx is an affectionate cat that, contrary to popular belief, relishes being cuddled. It is warm and soft to the touch, its skin feeling like fine suede leather, and because it is unprotected by fur the skin is easily damaged by rough or careless handling. Understandably, the Sphynx is an 'indoor cat', which must not be allowed to get cold, and when it is outside it must be carefully supervised. It will actively seek out warm, snug places and needs comparatively more food than other cats in order to generate sufficient energy to keep warm. This cat should not be exposed to sunlight outdoors for too long as it can easily become sunburned.

Uniquely among cats, the Sphynx sweats and, consequently, needs to be sponged regularly and carefully dried in order to remove the dander that is formed. It should also be bathed from time to time, ideally once a week. Although Sphynx cats are often said to be hypoallergenic and thus unlikely to cause reactions in people who are sensitive to contact with cats, this is not strictly true (see page 147).

One other unusual fact about the Sphynx is that its kittens' eyes open early, sometimes on the day they are born.

Don Sphynx
Resilient and sociable

Also known as Don Hairless, Russian Hairless, Don Bald Cat, Donsky and Donskoy

Size small to medium
Weight 2.5–5.5 kg (5¹/₂–12 lb)
Coat three types, which are progressively more hairy: nude (suede-like), velour (flock-like) and brush (fine and wiry)
Lifespan 10+ years
Country of origin Russia

Colours any
Eyes any colour

This hairless cat breed has only been around for just over 20 years. A cat breeder in the town of Rostov, on the River Don, came across Varya, a hairless female. She was mated with a mixed-breed cat, and the resulting litter was hairless. One of the litter, a black female, was then bred with European and domestic Shorthairs, so creating the foundation of the Don Sphynx breed.

The Don Sphynx is actually a strong, resilient animal. Adults are completely hairless but youngsters under two years old may have some short fur on the head.

These are loving and sociable cats, which, understandably, are drawn to warm places and relish being cuddled. They are indoor cats, and they need careful attention from their owner because they have no fur to protect them against cold or wet weather. They are more susceptible to injuries than other cats. In summer, if allowed outdoors, their owner must care that they do not get sunburned.

Peterbald

Friendly and voracious

Size small to medium
Weight 2.5–5.5 kg (5¹/₂–12 lb)
Coat in three types as the Don
Sphynx (see opposite)
Lifespan 10+ years
Country of origin Russia

Colours any
Eyes green-gold; blue in Colourpoint varieties

This breed arrived in 1994 from the crossing
of Don Sphynx cats with Oriental Shorthairs
in St Petersburg, Russia.

Sturdy and elegant, the Peterbald has
a longer, more fine-boned body than the
Don Sphynx and a more wedge-shaped
head. The completely bald or nude variety
feels rather sticky when handled, as if the
animal were composed of warm rubber.

This is an extremely friendly, attention-
seeking cat, which gets on well with
children, other cats and dogs. Like the Don
Sphynx, it will find the warmest spots in the
house, and it adores being cuddled, when it
will gently pat its owner's face with its paws.
It has a big appetite and is very much an

indoor cat, which must be protected from
cold, wet and too much sun.

Due to its need to be kept warm and dry
the Peterbald must be an indoor cat with an
owner who can provide careful management.

Index

Acknowledgements

Many, many thanks to Trevor Davies, my editor and now an undoubted cat fancier, and all the team at Hamlyn for their remarkable professionalism. Thanks also to my bunch of elderly Birmans draped, as ever, across my desk and computer, and producing, as I write, regular typos in the text by placing their plump paws on the key pads. Are they budding editors, too? Their presence inspires me.

Executive Editor Trevor Davies
Senior Editor Lisa John
Creative Director Tracy Killick
Designer Janis Utton
Senior Production Controller Carolin Stransky
Picture Researcher Emma O'Neill

Picture credits

Alamy Geoff du Feu 24; Idamini 180; Juniors Bildarchiv 65, 83, 105, 117, 120; Martin Garnham 43; Michael Nitzschke/Imagebroker 104; Petra Wegner 134.

Alan Robinson 45, 59.

Animal Photography Sally Anne Thompson 66.

Animaleyes Photography Melanie Whitten 108.

Ardea Jean Michel Labat 5, 187; John Daniels 133.

Dorling Kindersley 122–3; Dave King 23 below, 54, 126, 131; Jane Burton 14, 22, 51; Marc Henrie 111, 128; Paul Bricknell 140; Tracy Morgan 15, 81.

Dreamstime.com Katerina Cherkashina 179; Lenor 186; Linncurrie 175.

Fotolia Callaloo Candcy 101, 162; Chris Brignell 177; Katerina Cherkashina 25, 174; Krissi Lundgren 115; Larisa Kursina 171.

Getty Images Marc Henrie/Dorling Kindersley 167

Helmi Flick 31 below left, 63, 113, 116, 118, 129, 169, 173, 183.

Kimball Stock Alan Robinson 138; KleinHubert 99.

Octopus Publishing Group Ray Moller 1, 2–3, 5, 6, 7, 8–9, 10, 11, 13, 16, 17, 18–19, 20, 21, 23 above, 26, 27, 28 all, 30, 31 above left & below right, 32 above left & below right, 35, 37 all, 38–9, 40, 41 right, 49, 53, 67, 68, 69, 71, 75, 77, 79, 85, 87, 89, 91, 93, 95, 107, 124, 125, 130, 132, 137, 139, 143, 144–5, 146, 147, 149, 150, 151, 153, 155, 159, 161, 163, 165, 185.

Photoshot NHPA/Gerard Lacz 127; NHPA/Martin Harvey 136; NHPA/Yves Lanceau 41 left, 61, 73.

Warren Photographic 47, 56, 58, 97, 103, 135, 141, 154, 31 above right, 32 above right & below left, 157.